WHATEVER IT TAKES

A JOURNEY FROM DEVASTATION TO DELIGHT

MELISSA CURTIN

Whatever it Takes

A Journey from Devastation to Delight

Melissa Curtin

2024 © by Melissa Curtin

All rights reserved. Published 2024.

BIBLE SCRIPTURES

Printed in the United States of America

Spirit Media and our logos are trademarks of Spirit Media

SpiritMedia.US

www.spiritmedia.us
8045 Arco Corporate Dr STE 130
Raleigh, NC 27617
1 (888) 800-3744

Books > Christian Books & Bibles > Christian Living > Inspirational

Paperback ISBN: 979-8-89307-060-6
Hardback ISBN: 979-8-89307-061-3
Audiobook ISBN: 979-8-89307-062-0
eBook ISBN: 979-8-89307-059-0
Library of Congress Control Number: 2024909080

Avoiding the Invitation

If I'm honest, at this very moment, I don't feel inspired to write one. single. word.

My feelings are telling me to wallow,
to throw a fit and fall in it,
to do what I want to do... whatever that is, *but not write.*

I have found plausible excuses over several years to not take this on, *yet* I still feel *compelled* to write.

"Write about what?" you ask?

Well, I guess the best way to put it is I've been learning a lot over the past twenty-plus years in my walk with Christ, and I can only say that God has put it on my heart to share what I've been learning.

I don't have a PhD in Biblical studies or any formal training other than what God has been showing me through His Word, through His people, and the circumstances that He has providentially arranged for me.

I'm guessing most of this won't be new to you; that is if you have walked with Jesus any amount of time, *but* I'm a firm believer in God's promise to use the comfort we have received in our struggles to comfort those in any struggles they may have.

And we ALL have struggles, right?

Sometimes, I don't think that's true because I'm judging by what my eyes can see, but I only see what people let me see. And well, let's face it ... we all like to put on a good show and make everyone believe that everything is great in our lives, even if it's not, and most likely, it's not.

But I suppose there are some who have picked this up who have yet to experience pain and brokenness and are wondering how this book might apply.

Honestly, I have no idea.

I'm just trying to be obedient and *finally* do what God has been calling me to do for years.

Anyway, my hope is that if you know Jesus, you will be encouraged in your faith journey.

If you don't know Jesus, and some crazy friend recommended this book, and you reluctantly picked it up, then I hope you keep reading.

Because you're likely wondering what life is all about,
why you're here,
and what you're supposed to be doing,
and perhaps you're wondering if God exists at all.

Let me just say He *does exist,* and if you're reading this, *it is an invitation from Him* to enter into one of the most dangerous, exciting, and anything-but-dull adventures that will take you into eternity with Him where you'll experience unending joy and pleasures forevermore.

Thank you Valerie and Denise for encouraging me to put this out into the world. So grateful for both of you and your part in helping me move forward in courage in this part of my journey.

TABLE OF CONTENTS

I   Disillusionment, Despair and Demolition

II   Rebuilding, Restoring and Rekindling Affection

III   Abiding, Healing and Walking in Freedom

PART ONE

Disillusionment, Despair and Demolition

CHAPTER 1

How This Whole Thing Started

"Whatever it takes, Lord ..."

NEVER did I think words prayed would have such a powerful impact on my life.

I guess I need to back up a little bit and explain.

I became a Christian in 1993 as a junior in high school through a ministry called Young Life. Though I had attended church up until my parents got divorced when I was five, I really had no religious background. Sure, we attended church on Christmas and Easter, but I knew zilch about God and less about Jesus.

After inviting Christ into my life, life began to make sense.

Wait, slam on the brakes, "Invite Christ into your life?"

What does that *even* mean?

Unlike every other religion in the world, which says you have to *earn your way* into heaven:

> Being a follower of Jesus means having a relationship
> with the One who lived A PERFECT LIFE
> and died in my place,
> and YOUR PLACE, on the cross.
> He exchanges our sin and failures with His perfect record
> so we can be with Him in heaven.

So, I had accepted Jesus' invitation to follow Him, not follow a BUNCH of RULES.

That meant I knew Who created me and that He had a plan for my life. What that plan was, I wasn't sure, but He had a plan. I got involved in the campaigner group, a Bible study for other high school students who had come to know Christ through Young Life. My life was transformed. Old things had passed, and new things had come. Yet I still had a lot of questions. And though I didn't know it at the time, my worldview was still very much of the world.

I went to college as a baby Christian and felt invincible. Nothing would cause me to stumble. Well, stumble I did, and hard. I had been recruited to play catcher in softball at a small school in North Carolina and received an athletic scholarship. I liked most of my teammates and quickly made some strong friendships. I quickly fell into spending time with a couple of the upperclassmen, who also participated in the Fellowship of Christian Athletes.

After not much time at all, I began spending the majority of my time with one of the senior girls. I didn't really think much of it. I just knew she was fun, and there was a bit of a thrill in being accepted by a senior teammate. Little did I know, I was about to enter into one of the most difficult seasons of my life. Only after a few months of being at school, I was seduced into an abusive relationship with this teammate. Devastated and beside myself, I knew it was wrong and wanted to get out. Yet the pull of the relationship was too great.

I was living a double life and could not escape. Yet, I had confessed this to a close friend back home shortly after it began, and on a trip home during the holidays, she confronted me in love and encouraged me to tell my parents (Mom and Rich). I did, and that was the beginning of a very long road to break free from the stronghold the relationship had on me.

The fallout proved to be more substantial than I first realized. Following those years, I struggled with depression and fear that one day, someone would find out what happened and judge me for it. I graduated and moved back to my hometown, got a job, started volunteering with Young Life, and moved in with some old friends, but something was wrong. I still carried the shame of my experience at college and "knew" that if anyone found out, they would run for the hills.

Through a series of events, God led me to move back to North Carolina after being in St. Louis for a year and a half. I moved in with a good friend from college, got a job working with student-athletes at North Carolina State, and shortly after arrival, was approached and asked to consider volunteering with the student ministry group, Athletes in Action.

In a casual interview with the director, my abuse history came out. I had *intentionally* left out the part about it being a teammate who had abused me and secretly hoped that he would assume it was a guy. But to my surprise, he asked if my abuser was a guy or a girl. To my shock and amazement, after I revealed my abuser was a teammate, he didn't even flinch.

In fact, the response I heard was: *that God could really use my testimony with the female athletes at State who were experiencing similar things and needed hope.* That was the first step among many to escape from my paralyzing fear that I was damaged goods and could never be used by God again. Yet, I was continually haunted by the idea that I might run into my former abuser around town and not know what to do. Fear consumed me, and the underlying question, *"How could God let something like this happen to me?"* played through my mind.

While desperately wanting to be married and being highly attracted to men, I still had doubts about my sexual identity. Thoughts consumed me, "What if I got sucked back in? What if I *really* am gay?" The idea scared me greatly, and worse still, I had convinced myself that as a result of that relationship, God would never bless me with a husband. I wrongly believed I had ruined my chances. Though I would never admit it then, and I wasn't consciously aware, in my very core... I didn't really believe that God was trustworthy, nor did I understand the full extent of His love for me.

Though my heart had been shattered, my life's purpose was to have a good time. Sure, I studied God's Word and went to church, but what I really wanted was to have fun! A people pleaser to my core, much of what I did and where I went revolved around my desire to get others' approval and my fear of disappointing those I held dear. And in addition to that, my definition of being blessed meant everything was going well... no sickness, employment, friends, and nice weather were just a few of my criteria for being "blessed."

In early 2001, though I had a relationship with Christ, the reality that something was ghastly amiss finally became unavoidable. My emotions were everywhere. I was reading my

Bible and praying, involved in the singles' ministry at the church I attended, and had a good group of friends, yet I continually found myself feeling unfulfilled and straying from my daily time with the Lord. Much like the Israelites, who would constantly forget who God was and what He had done on their behalf, I would fall prey to worshiping idols, be disciplined, cry out to God, return to Him, and then repeat the cycle...

I found myself wanting a deeper and satisfying relationship with Christ and knew something needed to change. But what that something was, God only knew.

My exact prayer was, "Lord, do whatever it takes for me to walk close to You." I knew that was a "dangerous" prayer, somewhere in the proximity of praying for patience, but I knew I desperately needed a change. Little did I comprehend the wheels I had set into motion. God longed to do something marvelous in my life, and by His mercy, He waited for me to ask.

CHAPTER 2

By Any Means Necessary

"Daniel answered and said: 'Blessed be the name of God forever and ever, to whom belong wisdom and might. He changes times and seasons; he removes kings and sets up kings; he gives wisdom to the wise and knowledge to those who have understanding; he reveals deep and hidden things; he knows what is in the darkness; and the light dwells with him.'"

—Daniel 2:20-22 (ESV)

By the summer of 2001, I had forgotten all about asking God to do whatever it took to walk close with Him. Busy with work and distracted with life, I moved on and didn't really give it a second thought.

Oh, but God hadn't,
not by a long shot.

Though I had dated a few guys since college, none of them made it past four months. They were godly men, but they weren't for me. Though I wanted to be married, I wasn't really looking for someone at that time. How quickly that changed when a well-meaning and good-humored friend told me he thought one of the guys who was joining the Singles' Council, a core group of leaders that helped run the singles' ministry at my church, would be my future mate. Enter ... crush of the century. I didn't really know much about the guy other than the fact that he was tall, dark, and handsome with gorgeous blue eyes, and he seemed to have a heart for God.

It didn't matter though. He was *all* I could think about, and I began to pray that God would create an opportunity to become his friend. A week later, I received an invite to a Labor Day cookout at his house. Thrilled and a little intimidated, as I had never been invited to anything at his house or ever been a part of his circle of friends, I dragged my roommate along with me for moral support. I played it cool, tried to mingle with everyone *but* him, and continued to tell myself that he must be dating someone. While we did talk some during the party, I made it a point to not be the initiator–a great feat given my outgoing personality and take-charge attitude.

Next Sunday morning rolled around, and though we had the best intentions of being on time, my roommate and I were running late for church. With limited parking and seats in our ever-growing congregation, we decided she'd park the car, and I'd get our seats. The music had already started, and as I made my way down the aisle, I quickly scanned to find two open seats. Aha! I spotted two, and much to my dismay, I looked up and who but my crush "happened" to be sitting in the row. Surely, he would think that I intentionally picked that row, and that I was throwing myself at him. Thankfully, some good friends unknowingly rescued me by offering me two seats one row up. Whew! I had escaped, but didn't hear a word of the sermon. To my delight, he made his way over to chat following the service.

God repeatedly created opportunities to be around Doug, and answers to my prayers for a blossoming friendship with him became increasingly evident. Momentum continued to build as we had our monthly "First Friday" singles' fellowship event. Square dancing was the theme, and Doug and I ended up in the same group of eight and were partners to boot. We had a blast and definitely had some good chemistry going, and I reveled in the fact that this man actually perspired more than I did!

While I still really didn't know anything about him, infatuation had taken root in my heart. Yet, I was determined to guard my heart and not arouse or awaken love before its time (Song of Solomon 2:7b). Soon after, the Singles' Council had a beach retreat scheduled to develop plans and lay the groundwork for the upcoming year's ministry. While a good bit of the time revolved around planning inside the rental home where we were staying, plenty of time remained for playing ... and flirting. From going to the beach with just the boys while it was sprinkling ...

By the way, I *love* the beach.

Growing up in the Midwest can really make a girl love the ocean. But beyond that, every time I'm there, it reminds me of God's greatness and His indescribable power and authority to even hold back the waves.

Anyway, back to the retreat, to playing group games, and laughing a lot.

Then Sunday rolled around and we finished planning super early–around ten o'clock in the morning. A perfect beach day awaited anyone who wanted to partake, but there was only one problem: I had carpooled with another girl who had no desire to go to the beach. So, I asked the group if anyone was interested in going to the beach for the day. Of course, three guys were all about it, and one of them happened to be Doug. Needless to say, I wasn't disappointed. This also meant that one of them would be taking me home, and I'd be in a car for two-plus hours to get back to Raleigh. A few hours passed by, and one of the guys decided to head home, which meant that it was me, Doug, and Rob. Poor Rob. He quickly became a third wheel as Doug and I declined to go for a walk and became engrossed in conversation, covering everything under the sun. This conversation lasted the rest of the afternoon, including the entire ride home, as Rob had all but been forgotten in the back seat.

They dropped me off, and we chatted briefly about maybe trying to make the evening service, but we thought better of it and said our goodbyes. I jumped in the shower, and as I was getting dressed, I heard my cell phone ringing. I missed the call but had a voicemail. Of course, I checked it, and who of all people had called me but Doug. His message said, "Hey, it's Doug, I was just wondering ... well, just give me a call." I swallowed hard and returned the phone call, thinking the worst. He then proceeded to ask if he could come over so we could have a heart-to-heart conversation. My initial thought was, "Oh no, he's totally figured out that I have a MASSIVE crush on him, and he wants to apologize for misleading me this weekend." So, I agreed, and he came over later that evening.

The doorbell rang, and with an anxious heart, I answered the door. He came in and asked if we could pray. Doing my best to hide my confusion and concern, I agreed. He prayed, and I didn't hear a word, as thoughts of "an easy letdown" bombarded me. After we prayed, we talked some, and from what Doug said, I got the impression that he "just wanted to be my friend." Just be my friend?!? I was crushed. I certainly wanted to be *more* than his friend, so I asked if he still wanted to go get coffee, thinking he wouldn't want to waste his time on me.

As far as I was concerned, the door had been shut to any future with Doug in my life. Then the strangest thing happened: we went to Starbucks and had a lovely time. On the way back to my apartment, my understanding changed, as Doug said, "It's not like I want to hide that we're spending time together, but I want to take it slow." So, he *was* interested in me! He just didn't know what the future held and didn't want to get bogged down in the notorious singles' ministry rumor mill about who's dating who. That was September 15, 2002. Yeah, I remember it. He doesn't, and we have agreed to disagree if that was our first date.

The following Tuesday, I had planned to go out with some friends to go two-stepping, swing dancing, and line dancing at a local club. Dancing is one of my great loves, and one of my hopes for a future mate was their ability and enjoyment of dancing. Of course, it wasn't a requirement, but it was definitely on my list of desirable characteristics.

Doug called me on Monday to see what I was up to, and I shared my plans and threw out an invitation to join the group. He said he'd meet me there. No one ever told me how awkward it could be to take dance lessons with someone you really don't know. Though awkward at first, with a few bruised toes, Doug and I had a really fun night dancing with the group and with each other. Once he dipped me, I was done and officially "off the market" in my mind.

CHAPTER 3

Not Your Ordinary Courtship

"I adjure you, O daughters of Jerusalem, by the gazelles or the does of the field, that you not stir up or awaken love until it pleases."

—Song of Solomon 2:7 (ESV)

Things began to move quite quickly, and we established early on that we weren't going to spend our time watching movies or sitting in front of a television. We knew that in order to really get to know each other, we needed to spend time in more interactive activities. We both loved sports, so playing basketball and ultimate frisbee became a regular part of our time together. We also continued to serve together and do lots of group activities. Around November, we made the first trip to see some of my family in South Carolina. On the way there, we had another

DTR (define the relationship) discussion and mutually agreed that it was in our best interest to not use the phrase "I love you" or kiss until we were engaged, if we decided to take that route.

Now that may seem extreme, but because we both had been involved in physical relationships in the past, we knew it could be a major snare and distraction from figuring out if God wanted us to be together. We both felt that saying "I love you" should be a sacred thing guarded only for our future mates. A tall order, I know, but it certainly served its purpose in guarding our purity and keeping us from becoming sexually entangled. In addition, it really forced us to see if we had anything of substance in our relationship besides making out. Excuse the phrase, but you know as well as I do that the excitement and rush of physical intimacy can really cloud one's judgment and lead to terrible decisions.

Our courtship continued ... Doug came home for Christmas and fit right in with my family. And I knew he was "the one" God had picked for me. I had always heard people say that and really was quite skeptical about the whole thing. I mean, how could you *really* know? But, nonetheless, I did. And in the months that followed, I became increasingly frustrated with our decision to not kiss. Quite humorous, I know, but as a twenty-seven-year-old, that was just how I was wired. So, in early February, Doug and I had a heart-to-heart, and I shared with him how every time I was with him, I just wanted to kiss him! So, I'd just leave our time together angry and frustrated, not at him, but you get my drift.

In late March, we took a road trip to visit Doug's dad and stepmom in Charleston, South Carolina. It was nice to meet them and wonderful that they gave us the freedom to spend a night out on the town without making us feel guilty for not spending all our time with them. Of course, my growing frustration with not kissing had not abated, and so as we "enjoyed" dinner, I couldn't even really bring myself to look at Doug ... that's how badly I wanted to kiss him! We finished dinner, and being late March, it was still chilly outside. It was too late to catch a horse-drawn carriage for a ride around town, so we made our way to the waterfront and found a bench to sit on.

As we were sitting there and talking, with me looking the other way ... I know it sounds ridiculous, but that's how bad I had it for this man! Anyway ... he told me that he intended to marry me but *wasn't* proposing right then. My only thought was, "Great! Now I know he wants to marry me, and I *still* can't kiss him! Ugh!" He then ever so gently took my face in his hands, turned it toward his, and kissed me! It was the most wonderful kiss of my life and served to take the edge off.

We started talking about marriage details soon after and it was all rather surreal. I jumped the gun and asked my roommate if she'd be my maid of honor. And, her response surprised me. Instead of being excited for me, her feedback was that Doug and I were rushing things and she didn't think we'd been dating long enough to know if we should get married. That negative feedback from one of my closest friends at the time sent me reeling and catapulted me into a spiral of doubt about everything. That conversation, though irritating and painful, caused me to reevaluate my potential mate selection and also opened the door for unanswered questions about my sexual identity to be addressed.

Of course, the level of importance and validity that I placed on my friend's counsel was disproportionate and was driven by my approval addiction, but it served its purpose nonetheless. As Doug and I were St. Louis-bound over Easter break for him to ask for my hand in marriage, I flipped out. I couldn't handle it and wasn't ready. Just when I thought I knew he was "the one," doubt like waves of the sea swept me off my feet. Little did I know that he already had a ring purchased, and he had made a plan with my parents to propose. Nonetheless, we went to St. Louis, and he asked both sets of parents for permission to marry me. But by God's grace, he did not propose.

The year went on, and we continued to date. We had our share of ups and downs. I went through some counseling to address my concerns around my sexual identity, and he stuck by me. Several times, I tried to push him away with the argument that he deserved better than me and that I was too much of a mess to marry, but he stayed and shared over and over again that he was certain that God had called him to marry me. I didn't think I deserved such a kind-hearted man and couldn't grasp his perseverance.

Whenever we had talked about getting engaged, I had made it clear to Doug that I would prefer for it to just be the two of us. We had been around other couples when they got engaged and that really wasn't what I desired. So, when we made plans to go to the Hebron Rock Colony and Grandfather Mountain for a day trip with another couple with whom we'd been trying to plan something for months, I didn't think twice about the possibility that he might propose. Now the Hebron Rock Colony (a fabulous spot near Banner Elk, North Carolina) held special significance for us because we were returning to the location of our very first day trip together. Hiking its huge boulders and enjoying its waterfalls early in our courtship, and sharing our common love of the great outdoors and God's creation made it extra special. But I still wasn't thinking that he might pop the question there, and he didn't. He later told me there were too many people around.

After hiking the boulders at Hebron, we made our way over to Grandfather Mountain. It was pretty crowded there, too, but we made our way over the suspension bridge to enjoy the fall colors and take in the glorious view. Laura, Andy, and I ventured down to a little outcropping, and Doug fell behind a bit. We didn't think twice about it as he seemed very pensive, but I was joking with them about the possibility that he might be praying about asking me to marry him. Ha! Yeah right, no way, not with them with us. So we wrapped up our time at

Grandfather Mountain and started along the walkway back to the car. As we were walking, Doug asked Andy if he could hold our coats and led me off the path, past a sign that very clearly forbade entering the natural area.

As he held my hand and led me a little out of the way, my heart began to race in my chest, and I was wondering, "Could this be it?" We stopped, and he started telling me all these wonderful things about me and how he cared for me, and in the midst of it he said, "And, because I love you ..." An alarm went off in my head. Did he just say, "I love you?" I knew at that moment that he was proposing to me because of our previous agreement to not use those words until we were engaged. He asked me to be his wife for the rest of our lives, and I said, "Yes!"

CHAPTER 4

Trials Schmials

"Beloved, do not be surprised at the fiery trial when it comes upon you to test you, as though something strange were happening to you. But rejoice insofar as you share Christ's sufferings, that you may also rejoice and be glad when his glory is revealed."

—*I Peter 4:12-13 (ESV)*

Our courtship proved to be no less challenging than our dating, and at times, I wondered if I was making a mistake, and if I was all wrong about God calling me to marry Doug. Over time, it became abundantly clear that Doug and I were *very* different. Of course, our foundational beliefs were the same, and we had many things in common, but the adage that "opposites attract" could not be more accurate in our relationship. How much different, only time would tell.

We would often pray together, and many times—yes, many times—I would hear Doug pray something along the lines of, *"If we need trials, Lord, please bring them."* My natural internal response was, "What are you thinking? We don't NEED trials! Ugh!" Why on God's green earth would you *ever* pray for trials when life has plenty of them to begin with? Life is tough enough without asking the God of the universe to make it more difficult.

From my perspective I was perfectly fine where I was and really didn't grasp at the time that trials really could be a good thing. I had a very black-and-white view concerning trials: no trials, good; trials, bad. It was a pretty basic philosophy, but that's what I believed, even though I had memorized James 1:2-3 (NIV).

"Consider it pure joy, my brothers and sisters, whenever you face trials of many kinds, because you know that the testing of your faith produces perseverance."

Sure, I paid that verse lip service, but I didn't really believe it in my heart. My despair-filled attitude and depressed demeanor whenever even the tiniest thing didn't go the way I wanted betrayed my real thinking: trials were to be avoided like the plague.

Though I had experienced some very life-altering and potentially devastating trials in my very short twenty-seven-year-old life, I had not embraced them. I saw myself as having survived my trials and not made better because of them. Doug, however, had a very different view of trials. Unlike me, Doug saw the trials he had encountered in his life as the means by which God had drawn Doug to Himself. He saw the pain, struggles, and hardship as the path by which the God of the universe broke Doug's prideful spirit and enabled him to surrender his life to the Lordship of Jesus. Sounds familiar to James 1, doesn't it?

Aside from aiming to have fun in life, a very close second goal was to be comfortable. Of course, I didn't see that at the time. Most certainly, I was a product of my culture. The philosophy that I was entitled to an easy life permeated my very black-and-white existence. Although I knew that trials were to be expected in life, it didn't stop me from thinking that life was best when trials were absent.

In the weeks preceding our nuptials—yes, weeks, not months, but weeks before we were to be married—one of my bridesmaids, over dinner, shared her concerns about Doug and me getting married. She was concerned about my emotional stability and wondered if I was certain that I should marry Doug. At the time, it was like a slap in the face.

Our engagement was six months, and she had plenty of time to voice her concerns, but three weeks before our wedding? In hindsight, I know her confronting me was out of genuine concern and kind intention, but it was nonetheless difficult to hear. Truth be told, at that moment, I was not sure. I had so many doubts, and things had seemed to be extra hard, and we were so different. I really was thinking, "How in the world is this going to work?" I was far from comfortable following that dinner, and I sought the Lord's direction once again.

CHAPTER 5

My Stake
in the Sand

*"The LORD said to Gideon, 'The people with you are too many
for me to give the Midianites into their hand, lest Israel boast over
me, saying, "'My own hand has saved me.'"*

—Judges 7:2 (ESV)

Still reeling from my friend's words, and because I have a
tendency to care about man's opinion more than God's, I
decided to spend a day praying and fasting to discern if this was
a warning from the Lord or not. In my time with Him, He led
me to the story of Gideon in Judges 6-7.

Now, if you haven't read the story of Gideon, you should,
because it is a textbook example of God delighting in orchestrating

circumstances to clearly show the manifestation of His power in seemingly impossible situations for the people of God and for His glory. In short, Israel has turned from the Lord, and as discipline, an enemy country, Midian, keeps attacking Israel year in and year out. Israel is in hiding from Midian just to survive, and while Gideon, one of the Israelites, is threshing wheat in a wine press of all places, God shows up and tells him to go save Israel from the Midianites. After testing the Lord and determining he isn't out of his mind, Gideon decides to obey God's call.

As Gideon and the army prepare, they have roughly 32,000 troops. Then God has him whittle down the army to 300 troops! The reason: God wanted to get the glory. He didn't want Israel thinking they won the battle on their own. He wanted Israel to know beyond a shadow of a doubt that He was the One who saved them from Midian. And as I read the story, I sensed the Holy Spirit confirming that, yes, I was to marry Doug, and though it might look impossible, He was going to get the glory.

CHAPTER 6

"No Matter What...Trust Me"

"Cease striving and know that I am God."

—Psalm 46:10 (NASB)

Shortly after we returned from our honeymoon, things went south quickly. Not only had my best friend stopped speaking to me with no explanation, but it also was quite apparent that we had some serious issues to work through. Furthermore, six months into our marriage, Doug started experiencing severe back pain that impacted every facet of our lives. Literally, the bottom fell out of my world. Everything that I had expected and looked forward to in marriage was stolen, and expectations for my friendships fell painfully short. Many of the dreams I had dreamt were shattered and destroyed. Beat up and confused, I had entered into one of the most challenging seasons of my life. Clouds of despair threatened to overtake me, and severe depression began to set in as I felt betrayed by man and God.

Looking back, I know I felt that God owed me.

From my perspective, I had been living a godly life and was trying to please Him and glorify Him in everything I did. And, instead of reaping the benefits of being obedient, suddenly everything that I cared about had been ripped out of my life. Truly, it wasn't *everything*, but at the time it felt like *everything*. The enemy used this season to attack me with lies concerning my choice of mate. Daily, I was berated with doubts about who I had chosen to marry and the incredibly negative impact that choice was having on MY life.

I began to question whether God had really sent my friends to warn me and to prevent the current pain I was experiencing. Had I misinterpreted the "Don't be afraid" message from the Lord? Had He really been exhorting me to not be fearful of singleness? Words like "disaster," "colossal mistake," "trainwreck," and "wrong way" played through my head constantly. And, in the midst of the pain deep in my soul, the Lord began quietly impressing upon me one very important command:

"Sweetheart, *no matter what*, trust Me."

No matter how dismal things looked, the Lord beckoned me to trust Him.

CHAPTER 7

Stripped Bare

"For the director of music. A psalm of David. How long, LORD? Will you forget me forever? How long will you hide your face from me?"

—*Psalm 13:1 (NIV)*

Like a nice piece of antique furniture that has had its intricate details covered with paint, or any item that needs to be freshened up, all lives that are to be transformed by God's mighty hand, at times, must be stripped down to the very core to be prepared for their new identity.

The Lord's beckoning was just the beginning.

Was I willing to trust Him while I lived day in and day out in a place I didn't want to be, where "clearly" I had made a wrong turn, or the Lord had just plain forgotten about me?

I had hoped my friendships would be restored. I could find comfort there with those whom God had raised up to walk through life with me. At least, they could serve as a distraction from the pain of my marriage. But, over the months and eventually more than a year, those friends remained estranged. And tragically, I internally blamed my husband for the loss of those friendships, and like the Israelites who forgot the hardships of Egypt, I too forgot how I had longed to be married. I thought I'd be better off living the single and carefree lifestyle. Resentment and bitterness tainted my perspective and only exacerbated the struggles we were having.

In the meantime, Doug's back pain worsened. He went from occasionally not being able to do certain things to struggling to just be able to do the basics for life. His physical pain began to take its toll on both of us. At my urging, he made a doctor's appointment to see if we could remedy his pain and get on with our lives. After a series of appointments, injections, and a really terrible physical therapy appointment, Doug had decided it just wasn't worth it. The doctors and physical therapist he had seen had caused more pain and did not offer any real solutions. But, I was not about to let his pain interfere with our lives any longer than necessary.

Unlike Doug, I had always had exceptional PT experiences, and I reasoned that surely there had to be someone in the area who could help us. I began to research and investigate and got a recommendation from the counselor I was seeing at the time. The PT was a Christian and had a good reputation for caring for his patients and looking out for their interests. I put in a call to the PT to discuss Doug's symptoms during a lunch hour one day, hoping that I might get a call back, but I wasn't really expecting it, since Doug wasn't a current patient.

To my surprise and delight, Luke called me back in the middle of a business day to discuss Doug's situation. I immediately thought he was a perfect fit, though his practice wasn't on Doug's insurance, and it was on the opposite side of town from Doug's office. It just wasn't practical for Doug to go there. Or so we thought.

Soon after my conversation with Luke, Doug and I were invited to go to an engagement party for some dear friends. Not knowing any of the other couples at the party, we began to make polite conversation with the other couples there. To my astonishment, I found out that one of the guests at the party actually owned the PT practice that Luke worked for! Through our conversation with the owner, it became very apparent that God had orchestrated our meeting with the owner, and we quickly made an appointment with Luke.

After several months of PT, Doug was still experiencing an excruciating amount of pain, and Luke gave Doug a referral to one of the top neurosurgeons in the area. Surgery was not something either one of us was excited about, but we decided to meet with Dr. Garner to at least investigate the possibilities. In our meeting with him, it was evident that he, too, was not quick to rush into surgery, and really only performed surgeries when he was certain they would provide relief for his patient's pain. After a few appointments and trying different steroid approaches to reduce Doug's swelling and no results, Dr. Garner ordered some tests to try and diagnose what was causing Doug's pain. The results were inconclusive, and the film provided no indication as to what was causing the shooting pain down Doug's left leg. With no clear direction, Dr. Garner referred us to an orthopedic surgeon whom he frequently collaborated with on surgeries.

While there, we discussed several options, but ultimately the surgeon felt that the symptoms Doug was describing were consistent with pinched nerves, and he sent us back to Dr. Garner with a note to do the surgery. He reasoned the worst case was that Dr. Garner wouldn't find anything, but the best case was that some of Doug's pain could be alleviated. After a long and painful trial, Doug was finally free of his pain following surgery on October 31, 2005. We rejoiced that his pain was gone and looked forward to our life returning to some sense of "normalcy."

However, that wasn't exactly what God had planned.

CHAPTER 8

Relinquishing "My Rights"

"Do nothing from selfish ambition or conceit, but in humility count others more significant than yourselves. Let each of you look not only to his own interests, but also to the interests of others. Have this mind among yourselves, which is yours in Christ Jesus, who, though he was in the form of God, did not count equality with God a thing to be grasped, but emptied himself, by taking the form of a servant, being born in the likeness of men. And being found in human form, he humbled himself by becoming obedient to the point of death, even death on a cross."

—Philippians 2:3-8 (ESV)

While I had a fairly good facade in place, I was barely holding it together. My dreams remained beyond my grasp, and my resentment and bitterness continued to grow. On top of still not having the slightest clue as to what happened with my best friend, Doug and I continued to have MAJOR problems. In the midst of our ordeal with Doug's back pain, physical intimacy became less and less frequent, an area of our marriage which was already quite complicated because of our choice to go the natural family planning (NFP) route during our engagement. The hormones in the birth control I tried gave me crazy bad headaches and wreaked havoc on my emotions. So, NFP was the route we chose.

For background, if you're really not ready to start a family, NFP only provides you with a couple of weeks during the month when getting pregnant is unlikely. Combine that with the physiological phenomenon that generally, female libido is higher during the times of the month that she is fertile, and a flip-flopped scenario where I naturally had a higher desire for physical intimacy than my husband, and as if those two variables didn't add enough excitement, throw in the variable that both my husband and I had experienced various levels of trauma prior to marriage ... and voilà, you get the perfect concoction for the perfect storm.

Though Doug's back was better and his pain had been remedied, physical intimacy remained out of the picture. While my desires to be close to my husband and eventually have children were not wrong, they were all-consuming. To put it bluntly: sex and kids. That's what I wanted. And as far as I could tell, Doug was the only thing standing in my way of both of those dreams. As the weeks turned into months and months turned into years, disappointment grew to discontent, and discontent grew to despair, and despair turned into depression, and suicidal thoughts were not far behind.

Somewhere in the middle, as I was traveling—probably for work that I didn't really want to be doing because part of my dream was to be a stay-at-home mom—I was having a quiet time during a flight, going who knows where. And while I was studying Philippians 2, God spoke fresh to me through His Word. All along, I had the idea that having sex with my husband was my right. I was entitled to it. Heck, the Bible talks about not withholding yourself from your spouse, and the very definition of marriage is two people becoming one flesh.

Yet, as I read, God began to crack through the hard exterior of my heart. In Philippians 2, you see again that Jesus is God. By His very nature, He has the same rights and privileges as God, yet it says, "though he was in the form of God, did not count equality with God a thing to be grasped..." To be grasped has the picture of holding something really tightly. I was holding my rights as a wife very tightly, and because my rights were being violated, I understandably felt very hurt, betrayed, unloved, confused, ugly... the list goes on.

Yet, during that flight, I sensed Jesus saying, "Let go of your rights."

CHAPTER 9

Get Out
of the Way

"Cease striving and know that I am God."

– Psalm 46:10 (NASV)

I can't remember the year exactly. If I went back in my journals, I could probably pinpoint the date. But at some point, it became very evident to me that God wanted me to get out of the way and let Him work. And by "out of the way," it meant I needed to stop trying to fix our situation.

I needed to stop concocting ways to get my story to turn out the way I envisioned it being. I needed to stop trying to micromanage the God of the universe.

Yes, you read that right. Without even realizing it, I think we all have a tendency to tell God how our lives should look and hurry up already and do "the thing."

I've worked for micromanagers before, and it's not pleasant. More than anything, I felt like they doubted I would do what I said I'd do. Despite having a track record of responsibility and trustworthiness, the constant hovering and following up multiple times before looming deadlines made me irritated, mad, and honestly, on occasion, had me on the verge of quitting.

My attempts to micromanage the God of the universe reveal the core problem of my heart: that I really don't trust Him.

I don't trust that He has good plans.

I don't trust that He knows what He's doing.

I don't trust that He loves me and that He knows best.

The list goes on and on.

Thankfully, He doesn't treat me or get irritated with me like I do with people who attempt to micromanage me. He doesn't threaten to quit or throw up His hands in frustration. He has promised to never leave or forsake me and anyone who follows Him. And He created the universe and sustains EVERYTHING with His power. I'm guessing He likely knows what He is doing in our circumstances, even if we can't understand the why or the how.

And by guessing, I mean my head and my heart have a continual battle over whether I will believe my emotions and feelings or His Word to be the absolute authority on any matter. If you're like me, your emotions cannot be trusted. Take a breath, remember who He is, and that He always—ALWAYS—keeps His promises and ALWAYS has a plan, and a good plan at that.

CHAPTER 10

Thankful ALL the Time?

"Give thanks in ALL circumstances for this is God's will for you in Christ Jesus."

– 1 Thessalonians 5:18 (NIV)

We live in a culture of looking forward and looking back, wishing we were where we used to be or wishing we were where we want to be, but aren't yet. The problem with that approach is that we can never enjoy the moment we're in at present.

For a long, long time, I believed if God just healed my marriage, everything would be alright. I would be happy and life would be good. But, that thinking directly goes against what we see in God's Word. It says, "give thanks in ALL circumstances," not when your circumstances align with what you expected or desired they be. Hmmm... Problematic right?

But, here's the thing: in this fallen world we live in, there will always be someone or something that doesn't meet our expectations.

The other side of that same coin is that whatever is going on right now in your life is God's will for you in Christ Jesus. What the heck?

Well, it's true. The hard boss, difficult spouse, pay raise, unwanted diagnosis, season of peace ... ALL of it is God's will for you. So, we can give thanks.

So, my encouragement to all of us, including me, is to keep giving thanks. Even if that something is small, it helps tune our hearts to God and what He may be doing in our lives. An example from today: I had a doctor's appointment, and once back into my room, I waited nearly an hour past my scheduled time. Truth be told, I had the afternoon off and felt like my time was being wasted, and annoyance became my middle name. When my doc came in, he apologized and explained that the guy before me had a lot of questions. Hmm, so this doc actually takes time to listen to his patients. Ok, maybe that's an acceptable reason for the delay. After he listened to me closely and we decided on a treatment plan, I went on my way, thankful to have a remedy for my ailing tendonitis.

Despite being annoyed, at some point I actually thanked Jesus for keeping me there for whatever reason He deemed necessary. Maybe I would have gotten in a wreck, or maybe He just wanted to give me a chance to say thanks for making me wait. Whatever the reason, His direction can't be more clear. We need to give thanks all the time.

My Greatest Desire

"Whom do I have in Heaven but you O Lord, and Earth has nothing I desire beside You."

—*Psalm 73:4 (ESV)*

I have to say, Psalm 73 is one of my favorites. It's real, raw, and authentic. The Psalmist, like me, has a choice to make. He sees the prosperity of those around him who do not fear the Lord. They seem like they have no troubles. From his limited perspective, it does not matter if the wicked fear the Lord; they seem to be carefree. On the verge of despair and contemplating abandoning his faith, he enters into the presence of the Lord. Upon approaching the Lord, the wicked's fate becomes plain to him. The Lord kindly reminds him that the wicked's prosperity remains temporary. God is just, and He will hold the wicked accountable. As his heart softens, he praises God for His goodness and altogether worthiness. With his perspective righted, he has the ability to praise the Lord.

A skewed perspective has the potential to steal all our joy. And our enemy aims to constantly take our eyes off the One who is worthy and put them on our circumstances. Like in the Garden, he plants the seeds of discontent by questioning God's goodness and feeding us a slightly skewed perspective.

"Did God really say...?"

The Psalmist then calls to mind the amazing truth of God's willingness to endure his foolishness.

"When my soul was embittered, when I was pricked in heart, I was brutish and ignorant; I was like a beast toward you. Nevertheless, I am continually with you; you hold my right hand. You guide me with your counsel, and afterward you will receive me to glory." *(Psalm 73:21-24 ESV).* God continues to hold our hands even when we throw temper tantrums.

Just like parents who will not let go of their toddler who is kicking and screaming as they drag the child across the parking lot, because the parents know the child cannot understand the bigger picture. In mercy, He will NOT let go of us.

This psalm blows me away because after he recognizes God's mercy, he worships the King who alone is worthy. "And Earth has NOTHING I desire besides You."

Am I there?

No. Not. Even. Close.

I desire many things besides the Lord. But, the good news in this Psalm comes at the end.

"Though my flesh and my heart may fail, God IS the strength of my heart and my portion forever."

—*Psalm 73:26 (ESV)*

Though I fail daily to desire only the Lord.

Though I am constantly making idols out of every good thing God brings my way.

Though I forget He is enough.

Though I struggle comparing my circumstances with others.

Though _____ , He is faithful.

He is the ONE who will be the *strength of my heart* and enable me to persevere.

He is MY Portion.

That means He is ENOUGH.

CHAPTER 12

A Lousy Assignment

"So, we do not lose heart. Though our outer self is wasting away, our inner self is being renewed day by day. For this light momentary affliction is preparing for us an eternal weight of glory beyond all comparison, as we look not to the things that are seen but to the things that are unseen. For the things that are seen are transient, but the things that are unseen are eternal."

—*2 Corinthians 4:16-18 (ESV)*

As I sit here to write today, I think, "I have nothing of value to share." Of course, I know, or at least I intellectually assent to the idea, that I have something that may help someone. But, it has been nearly ten years and we are still stuck. Still dealing with a very broken marriage, I am crazy to be here. I am crazy for staying. If I was in my right mind, I would just call it quits, cut my losses, and move on.

Yet, I'm compelled to stay. Over and over again, the Lord continues to impress on me that this is the assignment He has given me. And my heart's instinctive response ... well, that's a crummy assignment. Yeah, that's probably shocking to some of you, but that's how I've been feeling about the whole thing.

Why me?

Why did I get this assignment?

Why couldn't I have the 2.5 kids, a healthy marriage, and everything else I deem to be necessary to have a happy life?

Oh, it's so complicated. But, then again, it isn't really, is it?

We just celebrated Christmas, and our pastor delivered a sermon a few weeks ago on "What does it mean to be blessed and highly favored?" After all, that is what Gabriel called Mary. "Blessed and highly favored." Because she had "found favor with God" (Luke 2:30b-ESV).

God chose to use her as the vessel to give birth to Jesus. Yes, God chose her, a poor young girl, who would be wrongly accused of adultery, of being loose and sleeping around, to bring the Messiah into the world.

God ruined her reputation for *the rest of her life.*

And her response is amazing. It's really, truly amazing...

"Behold, I am the servant of the Lord; let it be to me according to your word" (Luke 1:38 ESV). She readily recognizes and accepts her place as a servant of the Lord. There is no protest, no pity party, no 'Why me, Lord? This is so hard.' But why, Lord, would you choose me for this honor?

What is the difference between Mary and me?

Why do I lean toward thinking, "Why have you given me this lousy assignment?"

If I'm honest, I don't comprehend that He is worthy of whatever task He calls me to do. I just don't get it. There are moments when it clicks, but most of the time I am too shallow and too dumb to understand. There's a reason we get compared to sheep... one of the dumbest animals on the planet... just sayin'.

It reminds me a little bit of Frodo and Sam in *Lord of the Rings*. Truly, the task of getting the ring back to Mordor to destroy it and stop Sauron forever required endurance and long-suffering. And it required passing the hardest tests, and much of it Frodo had to do alone. I think the hard things God calls us to do have far more significance than we realize. Far more hangs in the spiritual balance than we can begin to imagine in the hard assignments we're given.

And when I remember that He is worthy of me doing whatever He has called me to do, it helps me to keep pressing on.

It reminds me of Paul saying, "Our light and momentary sufferings are not worth comparing to the future glory that will be revealed in us" (2 Corinthians 4:17 ESV).

I'm not sure how, but I'm thankful it's so.

PART TWO

Rebuilding, Restoring and Rekindling Affection

CHAPTER 13

Sweetest Birthday Gift

"The LORD is near to the brokenhearted and saves the crushed in spirit."

—*Psalm 34:18 (ESV)*

October 16, 2013—my thirty-seventh birthday—and so many unmet expectations of what I thought my life would look like by then. Married for nearly ten years, no kids, and no hope of kids in sight, and little change in our circumstances. Every holiday, every birthday, and every anniversary had morphed into not a celebration of a milestone or thanksgiving of God's blessings, but a mourning of unfulfilled dreams and unmet expectations. At least, that is what I saw when I took my typical inventory of my life and circumstances. Yet, God gave me a remarkable and exceptionally kind birthday gift.

As I sat there in the quiet of the morning pouring out my heart and reading the Word, it became very clear that my circumstances not changing were actually an answer to my prayer for Jesus to do whatever it took for me to walk close to Him. Plain as day right there in His Word, "The LORD IS NEAR to the BROKENHEARTED" (Psalm 34:18 ESV) [emphasis mine].

I clearly met the criteria for having a broken heart, and in my desperation for my circumstances to be different, it drove me to regularly cry out to the Lord to intervene. In the process, He opened my eyes to the knowledge of His desire for intimacy with me and His often unconventional and uncomfortable route to achieve it.

And, I may have been limping along, but I was limping along with MY God close to me, just like I asked Him.

CHAPTER 14

My Story isn't Supposed to be the Same as Yours

"But he knows the way I take; when he has tried me, I shall come out as gold. But he is unchangeable, and who can turn him back? What he desires, that he does, for he will complete what he appoints for me, and many such things are in his mind."

—Job 23:10, 13-14 (ESV)

If I'm honest, I have railed against the notion that my story is DIFFERENT than most of the people I know. Most of the people I know do not have issues the size of Mount Rushmore in their marriages. Sure, they have challenges, because all marriages— and frankly, all people—have challenges, but in my limited knowledge, no one I know is struggling with the same thing in the same magnitude that we are. And many times, I have found myself thinking and believing my story should be the same as theirs.

Comparing my story to others ... doesn't seem like that big a deal on the surface. We all do it, right? Whether it's a wardrobe, or family dynamics, or skill set, or talent or ... I often find myself wondering about others' stories and if they're better than mine. And, sadly, I often conclude wrongly that their story *is* better than mine, simply by virtue of a different story, or a more "desirable" story, or so I think.

Yet, who can know another person's story, really?

While I can know it from a friend sharing with me, I can never really know their story. And if I really knew their story, I likely would not want their challenges. My comparison with friends and strangers alike leaves me feeling like my story should be changed. And, more importantly, me questioning my story reveals a lack of trust in the One who has already written my story. The One who is good, and everything He does is good. The One who has written every single day in His Book. The One who loves me lavishly.

We see the negative consequences of comparing our stories in Psalm 73 (ESV). The writer has been comparing his story to those of the wicked around him. He makes conclusions based on what he can see of the wicked's circumstances. In verse three, he says, "For I was envious of the arrogant when I saw the prosperity of the wicked. For they have no pangs until death ... they are not in trouble as others are, they are not stricken like the rest of mankind ..." The result of the Psalmist's comparison is despair.

I've recently been thinking about all the people in the Bible and their stories, and I can't recall a story absent of trials.

I can't think of a single instance of a trial-free life, not one.

All the stories are filled with drama.

And, strangely and counterintuitively, I am encouraged by reading those stories and seeing God move on behalf of His people. All over His Word, we see trainwreck after trainwreck, and God stepping in to redeem and restore. *Why would I think my story would be any different?*

And if I really stop and think, do I really want a ho-hum story and miss out on the opportunity to know my God as a God who rescues or a God who reveals Himself to me? In my heart of hearts, I want to REALLY know Him.

In Job, the epitome of the story NO ONE wants, we see God reveal Himself as the perfect Author. He does everything and knows everything and does what He pleases. He is awesome, and no human brain can begin to understand what He does or why He does it. After his whole world fell apart, Job demanded God answer him for all the trouble He'd brought into Job's life, and God responded with about a hundred questions Job could not answer.

Job declared in 23:10 (ESV):

"But he knows the way I take; when he has tried me, I shall come out as gold." And, then he continues in verse 13, *"But he is unchangeable, and who can turn him back? What he desires, that he does, for he will complete what he appoints for me, and many such things are in his mind."*

I love the comfort and promises hidden in this passage.

He KNOWS the way I take.

He is not ignorant of what is going on in my life.

I cannot screw up my story.

He will do what He desires in my life.

He has appointments specifically for me.

Actually, many things.

I will come out as gold.

He has a set plan for me, and He will NOT be deterred from accomplishing it.

While my story may seem like a trainwreck to me, my heart is encouraged. I'm encouraged because there is the possibility God may choose to intervene and bring healing and restoration in the here and now. I am encouraged because this is light and momentary. I am encouraged because I know the One who is writing my story loves me like crazy and loves to get the glory, which means great things are in store for me.

CHAPTER 15

I Think
I Know Best

"Trust in the Lord with all your heart, and do not lean on your own understanding. In all your ways acknowledge him, and he will make straight your paths."

—*Proverbs 3:5-6 (ESV)*

Just about every week during preschool worship, we sing "Who Knows Best?" You may be familiar with it if you have kids or if you have ever served in kids' ministry.

Without including all the lyrics, the song essentially asks over and over, "Who knows best?" And then, whether it's how fast or slow to move, or what to do with our bodies or really any part of us, the answer is a resounding "God knows best!" Outside of the incredibly aerobic nature of the movements, it's sung with gusto. I'd even go so far as to say, borderline shouting and the quintessential cheerleader-like song which exclaims, "GOD KNOWS BEST!" in *every* situation.

Shocking, I know, for a kids' worship song.

And, if you've never heard it, it's worth finding it on the interwebs.

You get the idea. While preschoolers can learn and sing this simple song, it's packed with important foundational truths for EVERY believer. And for me, while I have been teaching little kids this song, God has been using it to remind me that I can trust Him, and He does know what's best for me. No matter what He asks me to do, endure, or say, I can trust Him.

While this applies to EVERY area of my life, I have really had to cling to this truth while I wait for God to bring healing in my marriage. I've been married for just over a decade now, and it has been filled with more challenges than I ever thought possible.

I know God is big enough and strong enough to take all the broken parts and make them whole.

And yet He hasn't yet.

And many times, I have felt like quitting. I have wrestled with thinking I misunderstood God's call for my life.

If this was God's calling, it'd be easy.

Right?

No, wrong. Very wrong, actually.

All through God's Word, we see a challenge to consider trials pure joy (James 1:1-2). We are encouraged to not be surprised by trials (1 Peter 4:12), and Jesus tells us to expect them. Could it be that God wants more for me than just a "happy, cozy life?" Above all else, God desires our hearts. He wants us to know Him in such an intimate way, and to understand He is our treasure, and He will use whatever means necessary to draw us and keep us near to Himself.

When I fully grasp the truth that God does indeed know what's best for me, I stop—

at least for a moment— (e'hem cosmic micromanager, anyone?)—

trying to call the shots in my life.

I stop wondering if what I'm going through is an accident. I stop feeling sorry for myself because I can rest in the truth that God is good and He is sovereign over every single second of every single day. He is trustworthy. And while my little pea-brain cannot begin to fathom how He is working all things together for my good to conform me to the image of Christ, I can rest. But, I've gotta keep singing this refrain to myself.

Because I forget.

We all forget, don't we?

As I think in my own wisdom, "This thing You're calling me to do … it's just too hard, or too impossible, or it doesn't make sense, or …" the refrain of this song "Who knows best? God knows best!" has been reverberating through my mind and heart, and it's helping me fix my eyes on the One who endured agony for me because He loves me, and He does know best!

CHAPTER 16

Molded By The World

"Therefore, I urge you, brothers and sisters, in view of God's mercy, to offer your bodies as a living sacrifice, holy and pleasing to God - this is your true and proper worship. Do not conform to the pattern of this world, but be transformed by the renewing of your mind. Then you will be able to test and approve what God's will is - his good, pleasing and perfect will."

—Romans 12:1-2 (NIV)

That last bit was written in October of 2013. It is now February of 2015. A lot, I mean A LOT, has happened since October of 2013. Yes, I've been putting God off, at least in regard to this assignment. Lent just started this Wednesday. I've actually never given up anything for Lent, but I know one thing for sure: God put it on my heart to give up sweets and TV for Lent. Sweets, I'm sure, are not uncommon, but yeah, you read that right, TV.

And since I'm not watching TV, guess what? I now have time to write.

But back to the TV thing. I've been noticing that many things that should break my heart don't. I have noticed an overall numbness in my heart, eerily similar to the heart of those the Lord describes as, "And because lawlessness will be increased, the love of many will grow cold" (Matthew 24:12 ESV), and I've been pondering why that is.

Why is it that I can watch a newscast about a murder, see violence and outright wretchedness, and not even flinch, when those things are clearly an abomination to the Lord? For me, TV has become a go-to method to tune out of reality, to tune out of the reality that I'm living in, and not think about my broken dreams and unmet expectations. But what I've also noticed is the more I watch TV, the more discontent I get with my own life and the more desensitized I am to things that should offend me.

I've known for years that I cannot watch romantic comedies. For me, it just stokes the fire of discontent. Watching these perfect people or quirky people have their perfect lives, always adoring each other, and if they argue, they make up quickly and are passionate ALL. THE. TIME. But you and I both know that's not life. I've recently realized that, for the most part, TV is just one more way for the enemy to speak lies into my life.

And I just passively absorb the garbage he's peddling.

It's subtle but powerful.

And it doesn't just have to be about relationships. It can be about our homes and home improvement, and if we just had a perfect lawn, or the right window treatment or ... Now, don't get me wrong. I am an avid DIYer. I love, and I mean that, love to build things, create, and make my home a nice place to be. But sometimes I can get so caught up that I cease to care about the things that *really* matter.

So, here's to hoping that spending less time binge-watching the next show will help give me the margin of time I need to really transform my mind and be able to identify the garbage the enemy is trying to sell me.

CHAPTER 17

Parched Desert Dweller No More

"Thus says the LORD: 'Cursed is the man who trusts in man and makes flesh his strength, whose heart turns away from the LORD. He is like a shrub in the desert, and shall not see ANY [emphasis mine] good come. He shall dwell in the parched places of the wilderness, in an uninhabited salt land.

Blessed is the man who trusts in the LORD, whose trust IS [emphasis mine] the LORD. He is like a tree planted by water, that sends out its roots by the stream, and does not fear when heat comes, for its leaves remain green, and is not anxious in the year of drought, for it does not cease to bear fruit.' The heart is deceitful above all things, and desperately sick."

—Jeremiah 17:5-8 (ESV)

This passage of Scripture has evolved into one of my life verses. I think God started using it in my heart when I was still a very young believer, but it has turned into an anthem for me. It contains such simple yet profound truth for how we are supposed to view our circumstances and how, if we will just trust our Father unconditionally, our whole outlook will change.

For years, I have been obsessed with God fixing my broken marriage.

I have pleaded, I have bargained, I have wept. You name it, I've done it.

And as a result of feeling like I didn't deserve this mess, that I had been faithful to God and had saved myself for marriage, I somehow deserved an amazing marriage.

It's the least He could do.

Yet, in believing those lies and raging against God, I was living as a cursed woman because I was trusting in man and attempting to make flesh my strength, and most certainly had turned at least part of my heart away from the Lord.

The second consequence of that curse is being like someone who lives in the parched places of the desert. Not just the desert, but the PARCHED places of the desert.

Could a desert get any drier?

Apparently so, and I can attest to feeling the parched places of the desert. The first consequence is huge.

It says you shall not see *any* good when it comes.

It doesn't say no good will come. You just won't be able to see any of it.

And that is who I have been for far too long. So obsessed with what I don't have, trusting in man and turning from God, my eyes could only see the thing right in front of my face that I was putting my hope in. I could not, for the life of me, be thankful for the countless blessings of God in my life beyond the brokenness.

Now, the sweetness of this passage lies in verses 7-8. Blessed or "happy" is the man who trusts in the LORD, whose trust IS the LORD. Trust is a verb and a noun here. So, I have the action of believing God to be good and trusting Him. But, then, the remarkable thing is that the very Person of the LORD is Trust. He is the very definition of trust, just like He is the very definition of love.

And when I trust in my Trust, I'm like a thriving tree that always bears fruit.

God has been doing a magnificent thing in my heart. He is slowly chipping away at the things that don't look like Him. He is slowly making me look more like Him and I don't feel quite so thirsty.

CHAPTER 18

We're Gonna Win

"And I heard a loud voice from the throne saying, "Behold, the dwelling place of God is with man. He will dwell with them, and they will be his people, and God himself will be with them as their God. He will wipe away every tear from their eyes, and death shall be no more, neither shall there be mourning, nor crying, nor pain anymore, for the former things have passed away."

—Revelation 21:3-4 (ESV)

As I have been wrestling with my circumstances and the pain they continue to bring, a movie from the early nineties, *A League of Their Own*, came to mind. If you haven't seen it, you should. But at any rate, it's a historical fiction film about the All-American Women's Baseball League that popped up during WWII. Tom Hanks plays coach Jimmy Doogan, and during the playoffs, when it looks like The Peaches will most certainly lose, they begin to make a comeback. But, in the midst of their comeback, one of the players, Evelyn's son Stillwell, begins marching back and forth in front of the dugout chanting, "You're gonna lose. You're gonna lose." And in one sense, it made me think of our enemy who is constantly trying to kill, steal, and destroy our joy, our testimonies for Christ, and our very lives. He's there on the sidelines chanting, annoyingly so.

"You're gonna lose!

Why don't you just give up already?

Your circumstances will NEVER change."

And, on and on he goes. But the other part of the scene revolves around Jimmy's response to Stillwell's chant. First, Jimmy pelts Stillwell in the face with a baseball mitt, knocks him down, and gets him to shut his mouth. Then Jimmy begins to say, "We're gonna win." And he doesn't just say it once but he says it repeatedly, and as the scene builds, he starts saying it louder and with more conviction.

And it dawned on me, that is my story, and your story, believer in Christ! "We're gonna win!" For all the times when it feels like things will never change, when we're in the darkness and desperate for God to intervene in our marriages, families, ministries, whatever your circumstance may be, we can say with confidence, "We're gonna win!" because we know the end of the story.

We may not win in those temporal battles. Those wins are never guaranteed. But Jesus has already won the war that will end all wars. He will wipe away *every* tear, and there will be *no more mourning!*

And, while the enemy tries to convince us to give up, we must remind ourselves:

"We're gonna win!"

CHAPTER 19

Flaming Darts

"In addition to all this, take up the shield of faith, with which you can extinguish all the flaming arrows of the evil one."

—Ephesians 6:16 (NIV)

I just found out that one of my estranged friends is pregnant. She got married more than a decade after me, and she has been married for only a few months, and she is pregnant. Now, we've reconnected on Facebook, but that is about as deep as our friendship will likely ever go. And my initial reaction, "Oh that's great!" After all, one of her dreams was to have a whole slew of children. But, not surprising, and predictably, the enemy made sure to make me think about how I don't have children, and how I should have children by now and how, well, you know how children are made, don't you?

Now, where the heck did that come from? I mean, I hadn't been dwelling on not having children recently and, in some ways, have actually surrendered to the idea of me likely not being a mom. Yet, from out of nowhere, my heart felt as if it had been pierced. And, indeed, it had.

I sometimes forget I have a target on my back because I belong to Jesus. And, actually, any of us who know Jesus or who are actively investigating Christ's claims become enemy combatants of Satan and his minions. So, they will use the most painful things in our lives to bring accusation, discouragement, and will ultimately attempt to kill our faith or potential faith.

The only way we can extinguish those flaming arrows that assault our souls? Memorize God's Word. How can we avoid unnecessary onslaughts from the enemy? Steer clear of the places, entertainment, social media, or whatever trigger you may have to reduce the enemy's ammunition. Share your struggle with a trusted friend or friends who will pray for you. And last but certainly not least, run to Jesus when you're under attack.

What a Refuge we have. Over and over again, Jesus has faithfully met me and has come to my rescue when I cry out to Him.

I am learning to be honest with the Father as soon as the enemy attacks my heart.

"Oh Father, you know I desperately want to have children, and this is hard news.

Thank you for knowing if I am going to have children or not.

And, if I am supposed to have children, You will make it happen."

My heart is growing in trust day by day, and for that, I am grateful.

CHAPTER 20

No Picnic

"We demolish arguments and every pretension that sets itself up against the knowledge of God, and we take captive every thought to make it obedient to Christ."

—2 Corinthians 10:5 (NIV)

If you were born before the year 2000, you may remember an infamous fast food slogan, "Your Way Right Away." The notion that we can and should get whatever we want whenever we want it, otherwise known as instant gratification, is pervasive. We're surrounded by it.

And that worldview, as catchy as the marketing team for Burger King made it, doesn't jive with how we have to live to spiritually thrive. But that's how a lot of us think our walk with Jesus should be.

And, well, there's literally not one place in the Bible that says we should expect that.

Though it does say He wants us to have a joyful and fulfilling life.

He doesn't just desire that we get by and just get saved, He wants His children to thrive and have abundant life.

So, how do we get abundant life?

Memorizing His Word is one step. The next? Shifting our perspective to align with the truth of God's Word.

But how?

Literally, *everything* in our culture says the exact *opposite*.

Many years ago, I can remember my friend and lifelong spiritual parent in my faith telling me, *"Melissa, so often as believers we wrongly believe life should be like a picnic. We're carrying around our little baskets, trying to find the perfect spot to frolic and play, and in reality, we're living in a warzone and under attack."*

Part of our warfare: taking EVERY.

SINGLE.

THOUGHT.

CAPTIVE.

Growth in Christ requires violent, intentional fighting of thoughts that oppose what God says in His Word. It's a GREAT effort.

It's dangerous.

It requires STRENGTH.

And PERSEVERANCE.

To be held captive paints a picture of being held against one's will. It's not nice. It's not letting those contrary thoughts hang out and mind their own business because they don't stay quiet for long.

We must absolutely take those stray thoughts that can act like grenades against our faith and wrestle them down and keep them down. If you're a fan of Jason Bourne, Jack Reacher, or any movie where the good guys go in and do whatever it takes to subdue the enemy, this is the spirit of this passage.

Maybe you don't picture yourself as a fighter.

Well, you are.

You *are* a warrior for Jesus if you know Him.

And it's time to train for the cage match. That is this spiritual life.

CHAPTER 21

Transformations in the Most Unlikely Places

"Therefore in view of God's mercy offer yourselves as a living sacrifice, holy and pleasing to God, which is your spiritual act of worship. Do not be conformed by this world, but be transformed by the renewing of your mind so you may be able to test what God's will is, his holy pleasing and perfect will."

—Romans 12:1-2 (NIV)

It's the beginning of 2016, and an amazing transformation has taken place. I have become a gym person. Now, that may not sound like that big of a deal, but previously, I would have characterized myself as someone who despised the gym. Having grown up playing multiple outdoor sports and just generally preferring to be outside, the idea of exercising indoors seemed horrible to me. But, in the first full week of the year, I have found myself looking forward to going to the gym. I've been thinking to myself, "I *get* to go to class."

In years past, I was somewhere in the vicinity of, "I need to go to the gym," or "I have to go to the gym," but this monumental shift has given me great encouragement beyond the extra pounds I'm hoping to drop.

But this shift did not happen overnight. Initially, I started going to the gym because I was "tired of being fat," and wanted to strengthen my core to help prevent back issues. It began as a "have to." I have been going to the gym for a couple of years now, and in particular, over the last three weeks, because of an extended break from work, I made going to the gym a priority almost every day. I made it a habit and intentionally planned to go to the gym. Things like packing my gym bag the night before, picking classes to attend in advance, and having a plan. All of that intentionality contributed to my mindshift about the gym.

To me, this shift parallels the picture of what God can do in any realm of life when we partner with Him. More often than not, His power is activated when we partner with Him and intentionally seek His face, spend time in the Word, and invest in friendships that spur us on to follow Him.

Of course, He doesn't have to partner with us. Like when He takes dead things and brings them to life, He makes the lame walk, and the mute speak. He gives sight to the blind. He parts seas and causes walls to come crumbling down. He allows the barren to conceive, and, and, and ... He can change our hearts to look more like His.

Nothing is impossible with God. Nothing. Let that sink in for a minute. And as if that's not encouraging enough, our God who set the moon and stars in place cares for us (Psalm 8:3-4). Our God who reigns supreme and sits on His throne (Psalm 9:7-8) inclines His ear to His children and listens. He moves on behalf of His people (Psalm 10:17). He can make me a gym person, for crying out loud. And He can make me more gentle and kind and compassionate. And He can change my marriage. Praise God, He can change my marriage. And He is waiting to incline His ear to you and move on your behalf. The God of the universe wants to move on your behalf. Soak that in.

CHAPTER 22

Good Works Prepared in Advance

"For we are his workmanship, created in Christ Jesus for good works, which God prepared beforehand, that we should walk in them."

—Ephesians 2:10 (ESV)

As I have wrestled with my calling, with the particular story God has written for me, which is far from what I thought my story would look like, I have found encouragement in the truth that God has specific good works He has prepared for me to do. Part of the "good works" He has prepared in advance for me is to love my husband even when he isn't loving me the way I would like him to love me.

He picked me. He appointed me to be in this marriage and live out my faith in front of a watching world.

As an aside, I think we all feel great about the notion of the good works God has prepared for us that we like and feel good about. Things like seeing friends come to know Jesus after years of hearing the Gospel, helping friends in their time of need, becoming a parent ... I'm sure you can fill in the blank with many examples.

But what about the good works that don't feel good and don't look good? Persevering in a hard marriage, being kind to the unjust boss, caring for the chronically-ill family member ... and the list goes on.

What I've come to learn over the years about the good works He's prepared for me to do–the hardest assignments seem to shine the spotlight on His faithfulness the brightest.

When friends and family members have to stop and scratch their heads and ask, "How can so-and-so do such-and-such and not be destroyed?" those questions can lead to conversations about Jesus. And they can also be the very evidence God uses to reach the lost souls around us.

Beyond that, He has prepared the good works in advance for us. The God of the universe has prepared them. Let that sink in. If you think about it long enough, it's really quite amazingly wonderful.

CHAPTER 23

A Burning Bush
at Pei-Wei

"Now Moses was tending the flock of Jethro, his father-in-law, the priest of Midian, and he led the flock to the far side of the wilderness and came to Horeb, the mountain of God. There, the angel of the Lord appeared to him in flames of fire from within a bush. Moses saw that though the bush was on fire, it did not burn up. So Moses thought, "I will go over and see this strange sight—why the bush does not burn up." When the Lord saw that he had gone over to look, God called to him from within the bush, "Moses! Moses!" And Moses said, 'Here I am.'"

—Exodus 3:1-4 (NIV)

It's June 2018. Yeah, this has been going on for a while now. God has not forgotten about me and continues to bring this notion to mind that He is calling me to something different than what I've been doing.

I'll back up a little. This month marks my fifteen-year anniversary at my corporate nine to five. I started there as an admin, and every year God has blessed me abundantly. In many ways, I have felt like Joseph where pretty much everything I have touched, God has made it great. Despite my not being super-passionate about the actual work, or rather feeling like I just need to be here because this is where God has put me, God has allowed His favor to go in front of me.

I work with an amazing group of people. I have been able to use my gifts of creativity and problem-solving to launch and execute award-winning campaigns, and just generally, the company has been abundantly good and generous to me.

Yet, *every* year, and I'm not exaggerating, things get slow and there is a lull in the work. I get bored and think I am not supposed to be here anymore. But I haven't the foggiest idea of what God would have me do instead. And, every year, I complain to Doug about how I'm bored and tell him I think I should do something else. But it usually ends with him convincing me that it's just a season and, for one reason or another, we decide I should stay. And the idea is to put it on the shelf for another year. But, this year is different.

For several months, things have been unusually slow, and the same desire to leave and do "something else" that I'm passionate about has been bubbling up in my heart. But, what is that "thing?"

I have a lot of what feels like random talents and skills. I love to work with my hands, encourage women, make people laugh, collaborate with people to find solutions to complex problems, brainstorm, fix things, play with kids, build just about anything, and on and on the list goes. But just one thing ... I don't have it nailed down.

So, this year, actually just a couple weeks ago now, Doug and I were talking over dinner about my work, my boredom and lack of passion for what I'm doing. In uncharacteristic fashion, I asked him what he thought I would be good at. After an initial half-joke about me installing solar panels, which I probably would be really good at, the first thing he said was, "You really enjoy encouraging women and discipling them. You could probably figure out your message and speak at some smaller women's conferences." He mentioned some other things, then God blew me away with what he said next. "You like so much variety. You probably need to work multiple part-time jobs."

Whoa, talk about a burning bush moment for the call of God on my life. I've been fortunate to have a handful of these moments. And, to have my husband be the one to suggest multiple part-time jobs made me stop and think, well maybe God does want me to do something different.

CHAPTER 24

What if
Doug Dies?

"Now the LORD said to Abram, "Go from your country and your kindred and your father's house to the land that I will show you. And, I will make of you a great nation, and I will bless you and make your name great, so that you will be a blessing. I will bless those who bless you, and him who dishonors you I will curse, and in you all the families of the earth shall be blessed. So, Abram went, as the LORD told him..."

—Genesis 12:1-4 (ESV)

As soon as I heard the words, "I think you should work multiple part-time jobs," it was like the heavens parted and I heard William Wallace shout, "FREEDOM!" Pardon the reference if you've never seen *Braveheart;* great movie if you haven't seen it. Anyway, my wheels immediately began to turn, and I started dreaming about what "the thing" might be. Then the strangest thing happened. I woke up a couple of days later, and the overwhelming thought of, "What if Doug dies? What are you going to do then?" kept reverberating through my mind.

Clearly, somewhere along the journey, unbeknownst to me, my salary had actually become my trust. Yes, I believed that God provided my salary and all of our needs. However, my irrational panic in potentially leaving my job for the unknown revealed how my heart had shifted to trust in my money and not in my God, who had faithfully provided for me every year of my life.

In that moment, I knew the Lord had put His finger on my comfort idol and called it out for what it was. And it became one more confirmation of Him calling me to trust Him, to step out in faith to the unknown, to "the land" He would show me. That's one of the most remarkable things about Abram. He did not know the living God or follow Yahweh, yet this unknown God shows up and tells Abram to follow Him to the land He will show him, and Abram goes.

He leaves *everything* he knows and goes to the country God shows him.

Of course, we can't tell from the narrative how long it took Abram to prepare, pack, and get all his people and things on the journey, but given other accounts (i.e., his obedience with Isaac), I'm inclined to think he obeyed the call of God quickly. I desperately desire to obey and move quickly, yet it seems I have some more planning to do before actually getting this show on the road.

PART THREE

Abiding, Healing and Walking in Freedom

It's been ... Ahem ... a few years since I wrote anything in this tale of God's faithfulness to me. It's now nearing the end of 2022, and so much has transpired in the last six years of my life. None of it, not one part, could I have guessed God would do. I don't even know if I'll ever try to get this published, but at a minimum, it will help me remember the great, great love of God for me. And, you, reader, if I do actually step out and get published.

CHAPTER 25

KT Tape Only Goes So Far

Journal entry: 12/22/19

"For 2020, I ask You to give me a heart that trusts You no matter how messy it gets. That is what you made clear nearly fifteen years ago. Would You help me embrace where You have me?"

In April of 2016, I got recruited to start teaching one of the group fitness classes I had been attending at the gym. Initially, I thought I really didn't have time to do it, and likely couldn't commit, but in true people-pleasing fashion, I agreed to try it and attended the training.

After all, I had been hand-picked by the group fitness director to teach classes, and I certainly couldn't let her down.

To my surprise, I loved it, and my participants loved me.

Well, I suppose it's not that big of a surprise given my affinity for being with people and loving to make them laugh. Nonetheless, as a group fitness instructor, not only did I get to work out and entertain people, I got paid for doing it. And when I went to the gym, I didn't have to think about the disaster of my life at home.

While I waited for God to move, deliver, heal, and change my circumstances, I threw myself fully into ministry and teaching group fitness classes. What started out as one certification quickly turned into another, and another, and another. It's fair to say I went a bit overboard. I had gotten certified to teach not one, not two, but *six* different programs over the course of three years. And in a normal week at the height of my fitness craze, I would teach/take anywhere from eight to eleven classes a week. And that was on top of my full-time corporate gig.

I'll just state the obvious: I unknowingly allowed fitness to become an idol in my life.

Essentially, I had taken a good thing and turned it into a god thing.

And at the time, I had a *sneaking* suspicion that I had allowed the gym to become too important, but that didn't stop me from attending and teaching as many classes as my body would let me. And, as Jesus would have it—*actually, He wouldn't have it.*

He wouldn't tolerate having anyone or anything in my life that I cared about more than Him.

Oh, the mercy of God, that He so often rescues us from ourselves.

So, His subtle hints started with a nagging injury here and another nagging injury there.

But I had KT tape, and LOTS of it!

Literally, it's as good as Duck Tape for hurting body parts.

But Jesus wasn't about to be outdone by synthetic athletic tape.

By the time COVID came around and we resorted to teaching classes in parking lots and remotely from our homes via Facebook Live, Jesus let my body give out.

As it turned out, I had major trauma to the second toe on my right foot. An MRI confirmed lots of high-impact classes and hyper-mobile joints resulted in the cartilage delaminating from my metatarsal and getting lodged between it and the phalange.

In layman's terms, my toe was seriously jacked up, and I needed surgery. I would be out of commission as an instructor for several months.

My outlet, which had essentially served as the primary distraction and stress relief, would be taken away. I sensed that my time as a group fitness instructor may be coming to an end.

CHAPTER 26

Unexpected Deliverance

"Then they cried to the Lord in their trouble, and he delivered them from their distress."

—*Psalm 107:6 (NIV)*

In early 2020, circumstances in my marriage had not improved at all. In fact, they had deteriorated to being completely hopeless. After hearing my husband tell me he didn't know if he could ever change, I gave up. I pulled away and stopped trying. As I previously mentioned, I poured myself into teaching classes at the gym, pursued friendship and fellowship with solid believers, and was trying to make it until Jesus came back or one of us died.

I prayed for relief incessantly, year after year, yet I sensed God wanted me to stay. Though I had every right to leave, repeatedly the answer was, "Stay."

It was Labor Day weekend, and after a pretty intense disagreement we both went our separate ways to cool off. While I was on my bike ride, I pleaded with God, poured my heart out again, and begged Him, "I can't do this anymore. Please free me!"

When I got back to the house, we sat down to have a conversation to hopefully "restore peace" to our relationship. As Doug started to talk, I couldn't believe what I was hearing. He gave me an ultimatum that included the phrase "separate." On one hand, I was dumbfounded because he was giving me an ultimatum. On the other hand, I was shocked because it seemed Jesus had finally answered my prayer with a "Yes."

After seeking Godly counsel, I spoke with Doug later in the evening and made it clear I was not OK with him giving me an ultimatum, and needed some time to think about everything he had said. A few days later, we spoke again, and he dug his heels in on his separation position.

Sure, COVID had been raging for six months, but I had no idea how messy things were about to get.

CHAPTER 27

Furloughs, Hurricanes, & Mariachi Bands

"Then Daniel praised the God of heaven and said:
"Praise be to the name of God for ever and ever;
  wisdom and power are his.
He changes times and seasons;
  he deposes kings and raises up others.
He gives wisdom to the wise
  and knowledge to the discerning.
He reveals deep and hidden things;
  he knows what lies in darkness,
  and light dwells with him.
I thank and praise you, God of my ancestors:
  You have given me wisdom and power,
you have made known to me what we asked of you,
  you have made known to us the dream of the king."

—Daniel 2:19b-23 (NIV)

I already had an appointment on the calendar with my counselor the following Saturday, and she agreed Doug had escalated our situation and it wasn't safe for me to stay at my house.

But God knew.

I distinctly remember thinking, *"This isn't right. Christian women don't leave their husbands."*

I was paralyzed with fear and doubt. I had no idea what was going to happen next. While I didn't want to leave, it was very clear I needed to do so for my own emotional safety. Thankfully, a dear friend, Sarah, was able to come over and help me figure out what I needed to take with me.

What transpired over the next several days, weeks, and months could only be explained with, "But God."

What the heck do I mean by that?

Well, I'll tell you.

All over the Bible, you see instances of impossible escapes, multiplied meals, dead people coming back to life, orphans intervening to save Israel, prostitutes hiding spies, wrongly imprisoned men rising to lead nations and save nations. ... The list goes on, and on, and on. In all of those, God's fingerprints were ALL over each situation. Mine was no different.

Beyond the perfectly scheduled counseling appointment, at just the right time, God parted the proverbial "Red Sea" in countless ways. Months prior to this final blow-up, my company mandated all employees take a nine-day unpaid furlough to avoid having to lay off people because of COVID. Everyone would not be working the last week of the year, but the other four days we got to choose. I just "so happened" to choose the week of September 14 to visit my parents (Dad and Lisa) at the beach. And I was going by myself because I had more vacation than Doug. Because I was working fully remote, I could work anywhere, including my parents' home. My counselor advised me to pack enough to stay away for a while so I could figure out what my next steps would be.

With the trip already planned, I was able to get away without raising suspicion about my intentions.

But it didn't stop there.

I decided to leave a day early, September 13, because I didn't feel safe staying at home.

However, there was a "hiccup." Hurricane Sally had parked right over my parents' city. So, as I was literally leaving my driveway and beginning the journey I did not want to make, my Dad called and asked if I could delay my departure. I, of course, couldn't delay, but wasn't ready to disclose what had transpired. I wanted to tell them in person.

Packing my things under duress and being completely unsure of what would happen next left me feeling exhausted and overwhelmed. I momentarily considered staying the night with Sarah and waiting until the next day to hit the road. After realizing I likely wouldn't get much sleep, I decided to break up the eleven-hour drive. I didn't know where I was going to stop, but I thought Charlotte seemed reasonable. And then I remembered my friend Libby lived in Charlotte. So, I sent her a text, and she "just happened" to be home. I told her I was coming to town and she invited me to stay at her house.

What I thought would be a night turned into four because of Hurricane Sally. The storm just sat there, dumping buckets of rain and wreaking havoc on the coast. While I couldn't drive, I could reach out to friends to ask for help, legal counsel, etc. During those four days, I had acquired a basic understanding of my rights according to North Carolina law, and God provided a temporary place to live with a friend of a friend upon my return to town.

Meanwhile, I had decided I should only communicate with Doug via writing, so he knew I planned to stop in Charlotte. But, I needed time to process everything before I let him know my intentions to separate for a time.

Hurricane Sally finally started to move inland, and her path lined up almost exactly with my intended route. So, to avoid getting stuck in nine hours of rainy driving, I decided I should stop near Atlanta and give the storm a chance to clear out before making my final five-hour drive to my parents. Thankfully, I had Hilton reward points available from my many pre-COVID business trips and found a Hampton Inn just outside Atlanta.

Within thirty feet of that hotel was a Mexican restaurant that "just happened" to be open during COVID, and they "just so happened" to have a live mariachi band playing that night.

Ok, sidebar, I love, love, love Mexican food, and love any kind of Latin music. In that moment, in the middle of my chaos, not having any idea how things would turn out, Jesus gave me that gift.

After several hours in the car and multiple phone calls with family and friends, filling them in on what had happened and what I decided, I arrived at my parents' house. Thankfully, their house sustained only minor damage, and they had a generator, which turned out to be a necessity because the entire city had no power.

I got my parents up-to-speed on what had happened with me and Doug and let them know I would need to stay longer than I planned, and they were completely supportive.

CHAPTER 28

Wedding Arbors & Pickup Trucks

"Now to him who is able to do immeasurably more than all we ask or imagine, according to his power that is at work within us"

—*Ephesians 3:20 (NIV)*

I had no idea what was going to happen when Doug found out I was separating from him. *Was he going to lock down our bank account? Would he change the locks on the house?* I kept running every scenario through my head, trying to determine what I needed to do next.

Now, my friend Sarah was getting married in October and I had promised to make her an arbor as her wedding gift. I had considered that I might not be able to do so because I didn't have access to my tools, but Jesus worked it out so I could build it at another friend's house. Yes, I think I've mentioned it before: I *love* building things.

But I had no idea what was going to happen to me financially.

And, I couldn't make her arbor out of two by fours. So, while I was spending time talking to Jesus at my parents' house, I asked Him to provide me with wood to make Sarah's arbor.

Have you ever asked God for something and forgot you did, then you remembered later?

Well, God didn't give me time to forget I asked Him for wood to build Sarah's wedding arbor.

About an hour later, my stepmom was like, *"Hey Meliss, the guy who used to live here left a bunch of wood up in the attic. Do you want to see if you want any of it?"*

Hello?

Double-take: *What did you just ask me?* Yes, up in the attic, in the house my parents had lived in for less than a year, they had wood. And it wasn't just *any kind of wood.* It was cedar and hickory: beautiful, lovely wood that would be worthy of being transformed into a wedding arbor.

So, I drive a Murano, you know, a "perfect vehicle" for transporting all manner of building materials. And I had a rough idea of my design for the arbor but nothing final, so I grabbed what I thought I would need and left the rest.

When I got back to Raleigh, I "just so happened" to have exactly all the wood I needed to build it. And I only made one mistake. That *never* happens on my projects. I'm usually a three or four trip Home Depot girl on most projects.

But then my friend asked, *"How are you going to get it to the wedding?"* My original plan involved building the arbor in three pieces, disassembling it, then reassembling it at the wedding site, but I sensed the Little Voice (you know, the one that nudges you to grab your raincoat or go back to get something you forgot, etc.). He's also known as the Holy Spirit, but I call him the Little Voice. At any rate, the Little Voice was like, "No disassemble," kinda like Johnny Five from that movie with John Goodman.

So, I said, "I have no idea how. But God provided the wood, so I expect He'll provide a truck to move the behemoth arbor."

Fast forward to the next day at church. I "just so happened" to run into my friend Bianca, who I hadn't seen in several years. I filled her in on the events that had happened in my life, and at the end of the conversation, she told me to let her know if she could do anything to help. So, I asked if she knew anyone who had a truck. And, well, you guessed it, she did, and they were willing to let me use their truck to move the arbor.

But, as if that wasn't enough. The distance between my friend's house, the friend with the truck, and the wedding venue was ONLY fifteen minutes!

I could just leave this snippet here and move on, but I have to stop and acknowledge the monumental importance of what happened.

Now, you may be of the mindset that the wood in the attic was a coincidence, as was the truck and all the other things.

But, what if for a moment you considered, what if it wasn't?

What if the God of the universe, who desires relationship with each one of us, was behind all of it?

Before the beginning of time, God knew I would be separating from my husband.

He caused my parents to move into their house in Alabama.

He caused the previous owner to leave wood in his attic.

He caused Sarah to ask me to build her an arbor before I knew what was going to happen in my marriage.

And, He caused me to ask Him for nice wood.

For me, this chain of events showed the great love of God for me as His daughter. And He *cares that much for you too.* You just have to ask for eyes to see Him at work in your life.

CHAPTER 29

Scary Decisions & Second Thoughts

"Fear not for I am with you, be not dismayed for I am your God; I will strengthen you, I will help you, I will uphold you with my righteous right hand."

—Isaiah 41:10 (ESV)

When I decided to separate from Doug, I did not want to do it. While I desperately wanted to be free from the very difficult circumstance, not one part of me wanted to leave my home and my dear friends. I didn't want to experience the fallout in my extended family.

None of it felt good.

Yet, it was clear I needed to leave for my own emotional safety. I sent Doug an email to explain why I made my decision and made my way back to town to live with a friend of a friend. She wasn't home when I arrived, and the reality of what I had done came crashing down on me like a tidal wave. I had willingly left my home and everything I had done to make it my place, to live with a stranger in a strange house. And not too long into the arrangement, I found out—with strange rules. And while God had been so kind and led me, I still doubted because my feelings were *so* intense.

Isn't that the way we go?

We feel, therefore it must be true.

Well, I have to say it again. Jesus is so kind. He knows how He made me with all these strong emotions. He knows I have a tendency to pay more attention to my body and what it's telling me than His Word or past experiences.

After being at the first house for maybe two weeks, things suddenly took a not-so-good turn. What seemed like the perfect solution *was very clearly not.* However, before that came to light, God did another crazy thing. He had my sister-in-law text me to see if we wanted to go to dinner. She had no idea what had happened. I, of course, didn't want to be the one to break the news to her, but I also didn't want to ghost her either.

So, I called her back and filled her in on what had happened, and without me asking, she invited me to stay in their home while Doug and I worked through our stuff. I was so thankful. I was even more thankful when not long after that conversation, I found out my roommate didn't want a roommate anymore and asked me to leave by the weekend. Before I knew I needed a place to go, God went before me and took care of me.

And His care didn't stop there. While our family wanted to be supportive, they didn't really understand the challenges we were facing. I knew I needed to set some pretty firm boundaries with Doug if our relationship was going to work and as well-meaning as they were trying to be, it became clear I probably needed to find another place to live. However, I really had no idea where I was going to go.

In the meantime, I reconnected with an old friend who used to live in my neighborhood and who had come to some of the Bible studies I hosted in my home. We met for dinner, and while we were catching up, she proactively offered to let me come to her house if I just needed to get away or needed a place to stay. The downside: she lived thirty minutes away. While I was not really interested in moving again, nor moving thirty minutes away, God had other plans for me. As I dragged my feet on moving, God allowed my niece to get COVID. Thankfully, her symptoms were mild, but that meant I couldn't teach or go to the gym for two weeks. It also meant I couldn't participate in Thanksgiving festivities with my community group. Despite her house being a significant distance from town, I made the decision to move ... again.

Moving in with Faith proved to be a bigger blessing to me than I could have imagined. She welcomed me into her home as a friend, and she had walked a similar road. We had many talks and meals together. I felt welcomed in her home. Like my in-laws, she didn't charge me any rent. She went above and beyond and was extremely generous in every way. On top of her generosity and welcoming spirit, she had one of the most excitable French bulldogs on the planet, Chloe. For my heart that felt like I was intruding or wasn't welcome in the first two places, Chloe's excitement and enthusiasm was a balm to my hurting heart. God knew I needed Faith and her little furball to help me begin to heal.

But I knew I could only stay until February or March because Faith was going to be moving closer to her job. Despite being a good distance out of town, I was able to connect with the families in my Providence Community Group. While I was the only single person in our group, it became a safe place for me to process life and receive the unique comfort and care the Body of Christ offers.

CHAPTER 30

No, You're Not Crazy

The Lord said to Gideon, "With the three hundred men that lapped I will save you and give the Midianites into your hands. Let all the others go home." So Gideon sent the rest of the Israelites home but kept the three hundred, who took over the provisions and trumpets of the others.

Now the camp of Midian lay below him in the valley. During that night the Lord said to Gideon, "Get up, go down against the camp, because I am going to give it into your hands. If you are afraid to attack, go down to the camp with your servant Purah and listen to what they are saying. Afterward, you will be encouraged to attack the camp."

—Judges 7:7-11 (NIV)

Flashback to circa April 2013. So earlier in this account of God's movement in my life, I referenced the story of Gideon and how God used it to encourage my heart forward in marrying Doug. Many times over the years I second-guessed that certainty and often wondered if the *"Don't be afraid"* part had really been, *"Don't be afraid to be single."*

Well, that's a question I'll have to ask Jesus when I get to heaven.

However, what I can say is that on multiple occasions, when I was at my wit's end and ready to throw in the towel, the story of Gideon would inevitably come up. Gideon is not like Lazarus or Jonah or any of those other well-known stories. It's slightly obscure, and literally every time Jesus caused it to be referenced, I was encouraged to persevere.

Well, April 2013 was no exception. I had signed up with a group of girlfriends to attend a Priscilla Shirer *Going Beyond* event in Virginia. The theme of the weekend hadn't been announced, but we knew it was sure to be encouraging, and we signed up with enthusiasm.

Sidenote, if you're not familiar or haven't read it in a while, you should read the entire story about Gideon in Judges 6-8.

Anyway, Doug and I had just had some very difficult things happen, and I didn't know if I could keep going. But, I went to the girls' weekend, hopeful God would meet me in the middle of my hurt. The first night, Friday, we all met together. Low and behold, you can probably guess what the theme of the weekend was ...Gideon!

In fact, Priscilla had written a study on Gideon, and her teaching that weekend would touch on the high points from her study. My heart could not have been more encouraged. And while I was there, God reminded me about wanting me to do a neighborhood Bible Study. And I had been putting it off.

While I had no problem being transparent with the women at Bible studies at church, hosting a Bible study in my neighborhood meant I would be giving the women who lived on my street a glimpse into some of the trials I was experiencing. The idea of letting my mask down, even slightly, terrified me. Now, you may be thinking, *"Why let your guard down at all?"*

Well, I had learned over the years in my faith walk that being authentic, in some magnificent way, had the ability to encourage hearts.

So, I pulled a "Gideon" with the Lord.

I'll explain.

That weekend, they were giving away a leader's kit with the Gideon Bible study. It included the DVDs, the leader's guide, and six study guides. I can't remember how many sets they were giving away, but it had something to do with submitting a story of what God had been doing in our lives for a chance to win. So, I said, *"Jesus, if you want me to do a neighborhood study, I'll submit an entry, and you have to make me win."*

Well, Jesus made my fleece wet and the ground dry. I won … gulp!

That meant I had to ask my neighbors to come.

I can't say I wasn't tempted to not do the study, because I was. But, the craziest thing happened. I asked my neighbors and every single lady I asked said, "Yes!"

I was blown away.

And after the first study they wanted to do *more* studies.

If you feel like God may be nudging you to step out of your comfort zone, you should most definitely do it! You never know what He has already been doing in someone's life.

CHAPTER 31

Faith like Gideon

"The wind blows wherever it pleases. You hear its sound, but you cannot tell where it comes from or where it is going. So, it is with everyone born of the Spirit."

—John 3:8 (NIV)

Now, circling back to Faith. After the Gideon study, the ladies were interested in doing more Bible studies, so I found studies we could do. And, each time, I would ask God who else he wanted me to invite.

On the second study I sensed I was supposed to invite the wife of the guy at the end of the street who had the two dogs.

I didn't know her, and I had only met her husband one time.

But I couldn't get it out of my head that *I had* to invite her.

So, with my little Gideon faith growing by the day, I got up the courage to invite her. Can you believe I knocked on her door and invited her, and she slammed the door in my face and told me she was calling the cops. No, not really. She said, *"Yes!"*

I couldn't help it. I had to throw in a joke. But, seriously, *this story gets better.*

What *I didn't know* about Faith and what God had already been doing was that her best friend, who was also named Melissa, had been challenging her to get back into a Bible study. And, literally two days before I knocked on her door she had committed to do the next Bible study she had the chance to attend. And, well, you already know the rest of the story.

Faith put her house on the market at the beginning of the crazy seller's market, and she got a crazy offer well above her asking price and had a contract within days. The crazy offer also meant she had to find something quickly or move into an apartment temporarily. She graciously offered to rent a two-bedroom apartment, but I didn't think that was a good use of her money. I had been praying about where I should live next, and while some friends suggested I rent an apartment, that didn't seem like a wise decision. I asked my community group to pray God would provide me with a place to stay.

CHAPTER 32

Listen to the "Little Voice"

"Since we live by the Spirit, let us keep in step with the Spirit."

—*Galatians 5:25 (NIV)*

Not long after I shared about needing a place to live with my community group, my friend Bianca and her husband, Josh, invited me to live with them and their three children, Isabelle, Gabe, and Grace. There really aren't enough words in the English language to express my gratitude for their love, hospitality, care, generosity, fellowship and so much more. Again, Jesus provided a rent-free place for me to live. And, as if that wasn't enough, I was only a few minutes away from work, the gym, and church.

The Thompsons see all their material belongings as blessings from Jesus, and their home is no exception to that mindset. They frequently have people live with them from time to time, and my stay wasn't unusual. I already felt like family because I had known them for so long, but they made me feel like it was my home from the moment I arrived.

And, as an extrovert living in the hustle and bustle of five other humans, my socializing cup ranneth over.

Oh, did I mention I have an extreme addiction to TV? Well, TV and movie watching happens rarely at the Thompsons. Instead, playing games, reading books, playing outside, and family devotional time filled many of the hours. And, while we watched a movie and TV show here and there, all of that time seemed to help me discern "The Little Voice," aka the Holy Spirit.

I wasn't the only one who knew about the Little Voice. Both Josh and Bianca had experienced the LV in daily life, and multiple times while I lived with them, we had times when one of us had or hadn't listened to the LV, and we'd seen the blessings of paying attention and frustrations from ignoring His subtle prompts.

Now, this may sound like some hokie hocus-pocus, but I can point to many times when I just couldn't shake a thought to do something, text someone, pray for someone, or bring something, and then that action has been a blessing to another human or me.

Have you ever had one of those moments where someone has heeded LV's promptings, and it was just the word of encouragement you needed, or just the thing you needed to get through the day?

I've been on the giving and receiving end of LV blessings, and my time with the Thompsons helped me to more deliberately pay attention and try to act on those prompts from the LV as often as I can.

One of the best examples where I was on the receiving end was the day I decided to financially separate from Doug. It was a very hard decision, and I felt like a colossal failure. His response to my request came from his attorney. While it affirmed my decision, my heart was broken. The kids had no knowledge of the specifics of my situation, and that day, of all days, upon returning to the house, I discovered the biggest chalk art message I've ever seen: "We love you, Miss Melissa!" It covered a good portion of the cul-de-sac and couldn't have been a more perfect time.

Besides practicing listening to and following through on LV's prompts, my heart had a safe place to process some wrong thinking patterns, distance myself from some unhealthy relationships, and take more steps toward freedom and healing. The day-in-day-out of bumping into each other in the kitchen and just living life helped to bring much-needed comfort to my soul.

CHAPTER 33

Blowing up
False Narratives

"Make your ear attentive to wisdom, incline your heart to understanding..."

—*Proverbs 2:2 (ESV)*

Have you ever had the experience where someone says or does something, or doesn't do or say something, and while you likely don't have all the facts, you "know" it had to do with something you did or didn't do?

No, just me?

Well, that art of narrative creating, and then living in response to those so-called self-authored narratives, had become a regular part of who I had become. Some of this behavior had connections to my childhood and having a strong aversion to conflict, but a lot of it had been nurtured as a survival mechanism for the emotionally abusive relationship I endured for nearly two decades.

I had learned to try and predict what would and what would not be pleasing to avoid conflict. While not healthy on any level, this narrative-creating had been woven into the very fabric of me.

While I lived with the Thompsons, Bianca gave me a safe place to ask clarifying questions—things like, 'You seem like you're irritated. Did I do something to bother you?' or 'I noticed you closed the back door. Was I being too loud on my team's call?' In those and many other conversations, I began to learn how to challenge my internal narrative that whatever thing that was happening was because of something I had done. In most, if not all of them, the action or lack of action had absolutely nothing to do with me. As silly as it sounds, I started to grow in my understanding and wisdom by asking clarifying questions.

Asking the questions of what else may be going on in someone's life or thinking through other plausible explanations can take the fangs right out of those false narratives and make way for healthy relationships.

Things like friends who have small children, have health issues, have other drama happening in their lives ... as much as we like to make everything about us, most of the time, it just isn't, and we can live in freedom and trust in our relationships. When we do have doubts, we can ask clarifying questions and blow the mess out of those false narratives or clear up misunderstandings. Either way, it's a win.

CHAPTER 34

Time for a Change of Scenery

"Whether you turn to the right or to the left, your ears will hear a voice behind you, saying, 'This is the way; walk in it.'"

—*Isaiah 30:21 (NIV)*

As I continued to live with the Thompsons, I sensed the LV telling me I would be moving soon. The thought of picking up again and relocating did not appeal to me. The Thompsons had been so welcoming and loving. The thought of going somewhere new where I might be rejected or feel like an outsider bubbled up in the periphery of my mind.

Yet, in May, I sensed the LV prompting me to attend a Providence Women's Event because my future roommate would be there. So, despite having overcommitted to too many things during the week, I decided to go to the event.

I ran into several old friends I hadn't seen in many years. We caught up and laughed and reminisced. Then, an acquaintance I hadn't seen since probably 2006 saw me from across the way and made her way over to say hi.

Stephanie gave me a huge hug and asked how Doug and I were doing. I explained what happened and shared about my current living situation. After a short time, she volunteered that she had two rooms and I could move in with her. I'm pretty sure my mouth dropped open and I laughed on the inside about what God just did ... again. So, I asked her if she was serious, and we decided we should meet and see if moving in with her would be a good idea.

We met for dinner, and I explained that I had sensed the LV leading me to attend the women's event to meet my roommate. Neither of us had RSVP'd for the event. Weeks before, a friend of Stephanie's had asked her to go, but she forgot about it. The day of the event, her friend reminded her, and she went on a whim.

After dinner, we decided we'd take some time to pray about it and see. In a follow-up conversation, she invited me to move in with her, and she would give me three months to find a house of my own. While a very generous offer, the thought of moving again and then maybe having to move again somewhere temporarily seemed like a not great scenario. The housing market had just started to go bonkers, and I had no idea how long it would take for me to get the money from financial separation, nor how long it would take for me to find a house.

After that conversation, I had serious doubts about moving from the Thompsons. I knew what to expect there, and I wondered what would happen if Stephanie and I didn't get along or if she changed her mind and rejected me. I explained my concerns to Stephanie, and she reassured me that I could stay as long as I needed to, and we would just talk about stuff if anything came up that needed to be addressed.

So, while I had a fair amount of sadness about moving from the Thompsons, God gave me a little insight into this particular move.

At this point in my adult life, *I had never lived by myself.*

I was either with my parents, with a roommate, or with a husband. But I had never lived alone, and the prospect of being by myself frightened me. Rather than having me go from living with five people to just myself, Jesus graciously intervened to provide a gradual weaning off of all the people to having one roommate and a sweet cat, Nicodemos, aka Nico. After taking time to remember how God orchestrated our meeting at the women's event back in May, I moved into Stephanie's house on August 1.

Once again, God went in front of me and prepared the way.

CHAPTER 35

Respite & Training Grounds

"If you then, who are evil, know how to give good gifts to your children, how much more will your Father who is in heaven give good things to those who ask him!"

—*Matthew 7:11 (ESV)*

God continued to provide the exact mix of things, people, and community I needed at the *exact right time*. While Faith had the ability to walk beside me with the understanding of someone who had been down a similar road, and Chloe served to fill my need for fuzzy companionship, the Thompsons rallied around me with their entire family to help me see a healthy family and love on me in more ways than I can recount. I had no idea, but Stephanie, Nico, and their home would be the very place God used to prepare me for my current season of life.

As I mentioned previously, I didn't really want to move again and didn't really want to move in with Stephanie. That had *nothing* to do with Stephanie. It all revolved around *my fear and worry of the unknown.* In fact, in all the moves God had me make, not one of them did I have an excitement or warm fuzzies welling up inside me. No, with each move, my heart, though I didn't know it at the time, began to learn to trust God in a much deeper way than I had ever previously experienced.

And, at some point, I think I actually stopped and thanked God that He wasn't requiring me to move daily like the Israelites had to do in the desert. I kept thinking how much of a pain it would have been to have to pick up and move every time the cloud of Yahweh's presence moved.

Though the Israelites likely hadn't accumulated as much stuff as I had.

At any rate, like every place before, Stephanie's home proved to be a very surprising blessing for my soul.

While the environment had none of the commotion and non-stop action I had experienced with the Thompsons, Stephanie's home proved to be the exact safe haven I needed to help me brave several big life shifts. Instead of an abundance of action, stillness overflowed within her four walls. While a good portion of that revolved around not having a small village in her home and her having a very active social life, much of it very much felt like a God-ordained rest stop for me.

While Stephanie traveled, I had many hours with just me and Jesus to ponder the future possibilities. At one point, I can distinctly remember grieving the prospect of living by myself, being all alone. Not having kids to make breakfast for, or a husband to dote on, just me.

And then, Jesus reminded me of two things.

One: while I felt very much alone in my marriage, He was always there with me and would always be. And two: though I wouldn't have another human to care for in my home, it would be an emotionally safe place.

As a single woman who has never been married and has a very full and satisfying life, I got a glimpse behind the curtain of what my life could look like from watching Stephanie. And my fear of being alone started to not be so big.

CHAPTER 36

Housing Holding Pattern

"My God will supply every need of yours according to His glorious riches in Christ Jesus."

—*Philippians 4:19 (ESV)*

B y this time, I knew how much money I would be receiving from our financial separation and started asking God where He wanted me to live. I very much felt like the sky was the limit, and I was willing to go wherever He wanted me to go. Whether He wanted me to give all my money away to ministry and move across the world to work with orphans, or if He wanted me to stay put in my current city, I asked for clarity.

At some point in time, not very much later, my parents (Mom and Rich) told me they had some news for me. They were going to move to North Carolina! And I had my answer on what city to focus my housing search.

While waiting to get my payout, I started to look at potential houses and got connected with a realtor through a good friend. But I didn't have my cash in hand. So, while I found a few I liked, I was very much in a holding pattern in the seller's market. And despite my fears about thinking I would never find anything that even came close to my previous house, God reminded me He already knew where I was going to live, and He was getting it ready for me.

And I actually wrote in my journal the things I was hoping God would provide for me in a house. "A wooded lot, decent yard with a fence, a ranch, wood-burning fireplace, good neighbors, close to work and life, an open floor plan, and a garage," were all the wish list items.

Around that same time, God did another amazing thing. My company decided to give out spot bonuses to all the employees who had stuck out the madness of COVID remote work upheaval and continued to help our company thrive. They based the percentage on years with the agency...Hello, 18% bonus! Needless to say, it was an extremely generous bonus, and getting it in advance of finding my home gave me a nice reserve of cash to tap into should I need it.

CHAPTER 37

Called By Name

"But now thus says the LORD, he who created you, O Jacob, he who formed you, O Israel: "Fear not, for I have redeemed you; I have called you by name, you are mine."

—*Isaiah 43:1 (ESV)*

Originally, this bit started as a rant about Valentine's Day and how I'm not a fan, for obvious reasons. But, that's not going to help me or you, right?!? Here's the more encouraging version.

Oh, how powerful it is to have your name remembered by someone. It evokes feelings of being seen and of being valuable enough for someone to take the time to commit your name to memory. It takes effort and a conscious decision to store it in your brain. When I taught group fitness classes, and even now when I attend group fitness classes or any social event for that matter, I make a concentrated effort to remember the names of the people I meet. It always made a difference and, most times, had people coming back to class because it made them feel seen.

Now think about the God of the universe calling *your* name. Like the most epic day of kickball and getting chosen to be on the team, right? But, instead of being picked for a lunchtime team for kickball, the very One who made everything, created and named the stars, well, continues to do so, I guess, because the universe keeps growing, so I hear.

If we'll embrace that truth, that you and I, if we know Jesus, can know Him more intimately than any human we'll ever know, we'll understand our worth and find rest for our souls.

Now that ... is a true Valentine.

CHAPTER 38

Flexing New Muscles

"Listen to me, you who know righteousness, the people in whose heart is my law; fear not the reproach of man, nor be dismayed at their revilings. For the moth will eat them up like a garment, and the worm will eat them like wool, but my righteousness will be forever and my salvation to all generations."

—Isaiah 51:7 (ESV)

While I searched for a home, God used Stephanie to help me begin to break some bad habits, flex my *"I'm not a doormat"* muscles, and challenge some wrong thought patterns that had become commonplace for me in my adult life.

I'm a Labrador retriever at heart. I want EVERYONE to like me and be happy with me. When that doesn't happen, I kind of panic. I question my worth and purpose. And, historically, I have obsessed about trying to figure out what I need to do to get back into people's good graces.

While I was living with Stephanie, relationships at the gym had taken a turn south and I DID NOT like it. After all, I was living as if my worth depended on the approval of my friends there. And, I had wrongly tied my identity and worth both to my role as a group fitness instructor and being a part of my instructor friend group.

I knew God was systematically removing toxic pieces from my story. And, I had asked Him to do it. But my comfort-loving, performance-driven self needed help from Stephanie to learn how to set healthy boundaries and identify areas where I was letting others determine my worth. Worth that, by all accounts can only be determined by our one and only Worth-Giver.

When I wanted to send a text to explain myself or set the record straight, when it really wasn't healthy or the right thing to do, she challenged me and asked me the hard questions about why I needed to and what would it accomplish. I had a pattern of giving other people power over me they didn't rightfully have, and that began a new pattern of starting to learn to be ok with dissonance in relationships.

CHAPTER 39

Hundred Dollar Apples

Meanwhile, Jericho was fortified inside and out because of the Israelites. Nobody could leave or enter.

The LORD told Joshua, "Look! I have given Jericho over to your control, along with its kings and valiant soldiers. March around the city, all the soldiers circling the city once. Do this for six days, with seven priests carrying in front of the ark seven trumpets made from rams' horns. On the seventh day march around the city seven times while the priests blow their trumpets. When they sound a long blast with the ram's horn, as soon as you hear the sound of the trumpet, then the entire army is to cry out loud, the city wall will collapse, and then all of the soldiers are to charge straight ahead."

—Joshua 6:1-5 (NET)

In the summer of 2021, Raleigh's housing market, much like the rest of the country, went berserk. Homes were selling within days of listing at thirty, sixty, sometimes hundreds of thousands of dollars over asking. In many instances, buyers from more expensive housing markets were swooping in and snatching up property faster than anyone could bat an eye.

As I continued to look for a home, I expected to have to make multiple offers and fail multiple times before I won. I had worked closely with my financial planner to figure out what price range I could afford and searched accordingly. While I had looked in late Spring, I had put everything on pause until I had my money. With money in hand, the search resumed. My realtor and I looked at a few, and I couldn't see myself living in them. So, we continued. And then I found a coming-soon property that had many of the things I wanted in a home. My realtor scheduled a showing, and as soon as I walked in the front door and saw the cozy fireplace, complete with a built-in firewood cubby, I was sold. Well, mostly.

As my realtor and I talked in hushed voices and other potential buyers looked at the property, we began to strategize and think through what my offer should be, given the market and what other comps in the area had seen.

I was completely smitten with the property. Nice, wooded lot on a quiet street in a great well-established neighborhood. The numbers I had rolling around in my mind seemed crazy. About that time, there was a video going around about one-hundred-dollar apples. *Ridiculous right, I mean who in their right mind would pay one-hundred bucks for an apple?* Of course, the video was poking fun at the housing market and what buyers were essentially doing to secure a contract. It doesn't translate well here, but I felt like I was buying a one-hundred-dollar apple and felt slightly insane.

While God hadn't instructed me to walk around the neighborhood seven times and wait for it to be given to me, I did have a huge undertaking in front of me and needed to figure out how much to offer.

After praying about the amount, talking to my financial advisor, and huddling with Kim, we decided on a plan, drafted our offer, and waited to hear what would happen. I'll spare you the suspense. I got the house on the first offer! Of course, my offer had to be substantially higher than asking to even get in the door and box out potential competitors. However, Jesus knew I would be buying a house in a berserk housing market and provided my surprise bonus and the appraisal came in over what I offered! Another praise!

My home would be ten minutes from everything in my life, on a quiet little cul-de-sac, and my prayer was that God would make it a refuge for me and anyone who came through my door. Next step was getting it inspected and setting a close date.

CHAPTER 40

Didn't See That Coming

"Every good and perfect gift is from above, coming down from the Father of the heavenly lights, who does not change like shifting shadows."

—*James 1:17 (NIV)*

My inspections were scheduled for September 1 and closing, Lord willing, would be October 5. So crazy. Such a God thing. My impossible need was met by the most gracious, most kind, and most generous provision by the Lord.

Not knowing a ton about older homes and things to look out for, I asked my brother Ron if he would come into town to be another set of eyes while the inspector was at the property.

He gladly accepted. So, Kim, Ron, and I met at my future home to find out what the home inspector had to say. Despite being built in 1983, there were only a handful of items that needed to be addressed immediately. Such a wonderful thing.

After parting ways, I was on cloud nine and thrilled to start dreaming about living in my very own home. Then I got a text from Kim, *"So, if someone were to ask if you were single, what would you say?"* What? Excuse me? What did you ask me?

I couldn't believe what I was reading. After years of being rejected, and feeling completely undesirable or unattractive, to have a man inquire if I was single was the last thing I expected. And, given my life station and all the lies I believed about my identity, I could only thank Jesus for such an unexpected kindness on top of such an incredible answer to prayer in providing me a home.

I, of course, had to call her and explain that, while I was incredibly flattered and downright encouraged, I wasn't technically single. My covenant, though broken, was still binding. So Kim, being the trusted agent and vault of my story, didn't disclose my current situation to my home inspector but told him to ask me if he was interested.

And lo and behold, don't you know that man had the courage to email me and ask if I was single and if I would go on a date with him! I hadn't been asked to go on a date in almost twenty years!

Ok, yes, I went on dates with Doug, but I hadn't been asked on a date with someone I didn't know. To be honest, I didn't even remember what he looked like. I did remember he laughed at my jokes and offered me bug spray when the mosquitoes found me outside of my future home. But beyond that, I was so distracted with the joy and excitement over my home that he didn't even hit my radar. And my radar was off. For nearly two decades I had trained myself to not look, not consider, not wonder what being with another man could be like.

So, I emailed him and let him know he made my day, but that I wasn't technically single. I very much knew divorce was imminent, but I needed time and was just trying to follow Jesus through the mess. I also said, *"If he wanted to still grab a bite/coffee/whatever after the dust settled, I'd be interested in meeting him."* To my surprise, he wrote back an empathetic and understanding email, told me he'd wait, and he'd be praying for me. All I could think was, *"C'mon Jesus, really? You not only provided me with the house of my dreams, but you literally dropped a Christian man into my house to inspect it and ask me out?"* I felt like Sarah when the Angel of the LORD told her she'd have a baby in her old age. In one fell swoop, God used this house inspector to communicate to me that I was desirable, attractive, worth the effort, beautiful, seen, cared for, adored, thought of, pursued, noticed and so much more.

And, living with Stephanie afforded me a safe space to be giddy about a man being interested in me. We sat on the living room floor, and I told her all about it. It felt like I was back in college, and I couldn't get over how God could have made my inspection day any better.

CHAPTER 41

Dragonfly Chairs
& Wayfair

"Therefore I tell you, do not be anxious about your life, what you will eat or what you will drink, nor about your body, what you will put on. Is not life more than food, and the body more than clothing? Look at the birds of the air; they neither sow nor reap nor gather into barns, and yet your Heavenly Father feeds them. Are you not much more valuable than them?"

—Matthew 6:25-26 (ESV)

With my closing about a month out, I started to evaluate what furniture I would be getting from my previous house and what furniture and furnishings I needed to purchase for my new home. I had done some window shopping at a few thrift stores, and knew I didn't want to spend a crazy amount of money right off the bat. I mean, I had just made the biggest downpayment of my adult life, and I was doing it all by myself.

In total, I only had to buy nine pieces to furnish my whole house. Nine things beyond what Jesus provided for me through my divorce. Talk about Jesus taking care of me! It might as well have been seven, because it was just perfect. Now, of course, I would eventually add more, update, etcetera, but Jesus in His kindness allowed me to find a really cute deep red chair and ottoman with gold/tan dragonflies on it and a coordinating red couch with gold trim. They were both at the same thrift store. The rest—my area rug and lamps—came from Wayfair, and well enough said, right?

One of the other really sweet things: with the exception of the guest bath, I really loved pretty much all of the paint colors inside my new home, and my old and new-to-me furniture would look incredible in my new space.

In previous seasons I haven't really given much thought to how much Jesus cares about the seemingly insignificant details of our lives, but if He decides when each hair of our heads' will fall out, I can imagine He also cares about providing for material needs like coordinating chairs and couches that don't break the bank.

Just recently one of my dearest friends has moved a considerable distance out of town to a brand new home. Of course, with a brand-new home comes lots of things to furnish and fill up. While she would have rather found a home within the city limits, housing prices meant she and her husband had to move further out where they could afford to live. However, they live on the edge of Boujeeville and Jesus has provided them with several really nice things at a fraction of the cost from the boujee-folk who "needed" to update. Needless to say, I'm thankful Jesus cares about the things we care about and He doesn't think we're silly when we ask him to provide them.

CHAPTER 42

Little Jim

During COVID and working fully remote, a couple of my girlfriends and I got the habit of having an "office morning" at the local coffee shop. It provided them a chance to get work done outside of their homes and afforded me much-needed people time while I worked. While my agency had started to have us back in the office a few days a week, they fully embraced a hybrid model, which allowed me to continue to have "office mornings" with my friends.

On one of our usual mornings, about a month after my divorce was final, Bec and I were working. Ginna couldn't join us because her kids were sick. God decided to encourage my heart with one of the most socially awkward humans.

As Bec, with her AirPods, and I worked, in walks this little man. His notifications were set to 100% volume and seemingly oblivious to typical societal norms. After asking all the nearby customers about why there was blue tape on the power outlet, he disappeared into the restroom for what seemed like an eternity. While he was gone, Bec had to leave to pick up her kids from preschool.

As I continued to work, the little guy came back and asked me if I was alone. Thinking he wanted to use one of the three chairs at my table, I told him he was more than welcome to use any of the chairs. After a short pause, he asked again if I was alone. I again, slow on the uptake, told him my friend just left.

And then he mustered up the courage to introduce himself, share how attractive he thought I was and ask me on a date. It went something like, *"Hi I'm Jim, I'm a former army captain and you're just so attractive I was wondering if you would go on a date with me?"* Now, Jim was clearly much older than me and I was definitely not even close to being in the headspace to want to date anyone, let alone little Jim. So, I told him I was flattered and knew it took a lot of courage to ask me.

He then proceeded to apologize for offending me, which he hadn't, and explain that all the pretty girls were taken. I told him he didn't offend me, and I kept working with him sitting in the chair across the aisle. As I was about to leave, he apologized again and emphasized, *"I don't look that bad for fifty-nine, right?"* Bahahaha! Fifteen years my senior. Not today, Little Jim. While it was a clear no, Little Jim was a sweet reminder from the Lord that I was desirable.

CHAPTER 43

Cheerios & Binkies

"Let us then with confidence draw near to the throne of grace, that we may receive mercy and find grace to help in time of need."

—*Hebrews 4:16 (ESV)*

On the morning of December 3, 2021 I received word early in the day that my divorce was final. While I mostly felt relieved, I also felt grief of the death of so many dreams. I felt ashamed I now had the label "divorced" to add to my story and wrestled once again with why the whole thing had happened in the first place.

Later on the same day, I got a text from a friend asking if I knew someone who had a mother-in-law suite or a similar set up so her mom and niece could stay. It's a complicated story as to why they needed a place for a couple of weeks, but nonetheless, they needed a place. And my prayer for my house was that God would use it as a refuge for anyone who came. I warned her that I was still in the middle of renovating my master bathroom and I was still living out of a dorm fridge and coolers. My fridge had died and everything was taking forever to get because of COVID, but if her mom wanted to come, my house was their house. Amy made sure I understood her niece was nine months old and would likely disrupt the peace and quiet of my home, and I told her I understood and they should come over. So, within a few hours, I had two new roommates: Valerie (whom I knew) and her granddaughter, Penny.

But God knew I would be feeling all those feelings and sent me comfort in the form of a sweet, sweet friend and her cuddly, giggly granddaughter. And they made the best roommates. Valerie Instacarted the groceries and introduced me to egg sandwiches with her go-to garlic salt seasoning and Penny left a trail of Cheerios and binkies around my house.

And Jesus did another sweet thing. In my excitement about having a wood-burning fireplace, I had an ENTIRE cord delivered to my house shortly after I moved in. And I COULD NOT wait to have a fire. Only problem, Facebook Marketplace Travis lied to me, and the wood wasn't seasoned. While the firewood I had delivered was NOT seasoned, aka would NOT BURN, Valerie had a giant pile that she invited me to use because her home wasn't inhabitable. So, we had lots of time to talk and catch up while we enjoyed many cozy fires.

Not only were they great roommates, but they turned out to be excellent cheerleaders and forewomen for my bath renovation. Having them in my house for those two weeks was such a kindness from the Lord. And for weeks, and maybe months later, I'd find a stray Cheerio under a couch or on the floor, and it just made me remember God's kindness in sending them to comfort me when I needed it most.

CHAPTER 44

I'm Allowed to Date?

"He who did not spare his own Son but gave him up for us all, how will he not also with him graciously give us all things?"

—*Romans 8:32 (ESV)*

Not long after Little Jim asked me out, and my divorce was final, I started thinking about my future and my desire for companionship. As I processed and wondered out loud if I even wanted to date, I jokingly took comfort in the knowledge that I could at least reel in a fifty-nine-year-old. Then Valerie said, *"Well, you have the home inspector, right?"*

I was dumbfounded. She was absolutely right. However, I had trained myself not to look at another man for nearly two decades. And, while my divorce was very recent, my heart had long since grieved the loss of my marriage.

A few weeks later as I continued to ponder if I should do anything about the home inspector, my friend Sarah enthusiastically encouraged me to email him. Afterall, I had left it that I would reach out when the dust settled, and I *was single* and for all intents and purposes datable ... *mind-blowing*.

Me asking a boy to go to lunch? What?! Somehow, even though he was very much a man, me thinking about dating took me back to that giddy high-school-girl mentality. So, I got up the courage to send him an email to see if he still wanted to grab a bite to eat. After all, it had been four months since he asked me out. For all I knew, he had moved on and found someone else to date.

CHAPTER 45

Whirlwind Romance

"I adjure you, O daughters of Jerusalem, that you not stir up or awaken love until it pleases."

—*Song of Solomon 8:4 (ESV)*

S poiler alert: we went on a date and another date and another ... and I. WAS. ON. CLOUD. NINE.

He literally ticked so many boxes that I had not experienced in the last eighteen years of my marriage. The joking, playfulness, carefreeness, and pleasantness of just being in his company. And, well the romance, what a treat for my heart, mind, and emotions.

We studied the Bible together, hung out with my people, started to get to know his friends and family...

I literally couldn't stop smiling and everyone noticed. The fog had lifted and we started having serious conversations about our future. Being a little bit older we both "knew" what we wanted and there were only a couple, e'hem, small, tinyish things that may be dealbreakers. Of course, I say that in hindsight.

I'll get to that in a minute.

But, after only a handful of months we were pondering if we should get married.

Full stop.

Yes, we were thinking of getting married. Being of the mindset and belief that God means what He says about the joys of marriage and all the things that involves, and both being on the more mature end of the age spectrum, and also, well, we both knew we could only contain our passion but so long, so it made perfect sense.

But, did it?

CHAPTER 46

Five New Roommates

"Every good gift is from above, coming down from the Father of lights, with whom there is no variation or shadow to change."

—James 1:17 (ESV)

M y parents' house sold in record time and they had not found a house in North Carolina yet. So, we decided they, and their three large dogs, would move in with me while they were searching.

While the quarters were tight at times and we sometimes had traffic flow issues in my tiny kitchen, having them in my home was an absolute treat. Not only were two of my most favorite people in my house, but they served double duty as live-in chef and handyman of the year. For a girl who has a hard time getting excited about cooking and also LOVES to do projects, this was a win, win, win.

Of course, Jesus knew what He was doing (eyebrow raise) when He had them move in at the height of my new-found romance. *E'hem, nothing says accountability like your parents watching TV in your living room.*

Beyond that, their time in my home reminded me I'm just stewarding this gift of a home for Jesus. He has given it to me so that it could be a refuge for anyone who sets foot inside its walls.

CHAPTER 47

People Pleasing Has Consequences

"For three years there was no war between Aram and Israel. But in the third year Jehoshaphat king of Judah went down to see the king of Israel. The king of Israel had said to his officials, "Don't you know that Ramoth Gilead belongs to us and yet we are doing nothing to retake it from the king of Aram?" So he asked Jehoshaphat, "Will you go with me to fight against Ramoth Gilead?" Jehoshaphat replied to the king of Israel, "I am as you are, my people as your people, my horses as your horses."

—1 Kings 22:1-4 (NIV)

So, about those tinyish things that I had rationalized as not being a big deal. Following our discussions around getting married we promptly decided to start premarital counseling to uncover any issues and get ahead of anything we might not see in the midst of the relational whirlwind.

And, let me just put in that plug now. Counseling of any kind with a Biblical therapist is hands down the best investment I have made for my mental, emotional and spiritual well-being. If you have been on the fence about seeing a counselor/therapist, I think everyone should do it. AND I especially encourage you to do it if you're considering marriage.

Ok, advertisement over. Anyway, without getting into all the things, over the course of time it became very apparent that we had some potential deal breaker issues. Now, I do have to say that it was several small things, that in and of themselves would likely not be deal breakers. BUT, when put all together and after praying that if there was ANYTHING I wasn't seeing—and that I didn't want it if Jesus didn't want me to have it—and exactly what Jesus brought to light, I knew, at a minimum, we needed to postpone our wedding.

For realz, I'm a recovering people-pleaser, and like Jehoshaphat, I sometimes don't make the best decisions because I'm afraid I'm going to hurt someone's feelings, or I want to be accepted, or... Jehoshaphat was a mostly godly king, but he made friends with the enemy. He essentially compromised on some really important stuff that led to Israel getting attacked and being put in harm's way because he chose to fear man instead of God.

With Jamison, I chose to ignore some pretty big-ticket items—well, maybe I didn't ignore them, but I didn't hold my ground on some very important things and decided romance and being wanted were more important. Of course, in the moment, I didn't realize it, and thankfully Jesus brought everything to light before we got married, but it had some painful repercussions.

Despite Jesus rescuing me from a situation that would have been utterly horrendous, I still wound up suffering the consequences of fearing man instead of God. And now I'm much more likely to fear the Lord instead of man because of the pain I essentially inflicted on myself.

CHAPTER 48

Miracle House, Miracle Timing

"My God will supply every need of yours according to His glorious riches in Christ Jesus."

—*Philippians 4:19 (ESV)*

As I took time to process my future and whether it would include Jamison, my parents got COVID. Thankfully, their symptoms were mild. However, it created much needed space and time for me. It also became very clear I needed to have my house back to myself so I didn't have the added extra pressure of trying to please my parents. Not that they were putting that on me. But, I'm a recovering people pleaser, so it's my default mode of operating.

As I dreaded the thought of telling them I needed them to move, I prayed about how I should bring it up and how they would take it. And, they also needed a house.

Now, months prior, I felt compelled to start asking God for specific things that only He could do. *So, remember how I shared that I had asked Him to provide my parents a house within five minutes from my house, sometime in March?*

With the housing market still absolutely berserk, it would be a God thing.

It was a Sunday morning, and I couldn't go to church because I had been around my parents who tested positive for COVID. So, after I watched the sermon online, I decided to go for a walk. But, rather than go my typical route, the Little Voice prompted me to go on the greenway. I had perfect weather and enjoyed the stroll through God's creation. As I made my way back home, I noticed a "for lease" sign in front of a house just two streets away from mine! It had three bedrooms and two baths, a fenced-in yard, and two sheds. I looked up the property, and it was renting for the same amount my parents would have been paying me.

When I got home I talked to them about needing space, and they totally understood. I then showed them the house, and within two days they secured a rental agreement on a house just a five-minute walk away. Whoa, Jesus! You know sometimes, I think God wants us to ask big things, just so He can show off and remind us of just how powerful and loving He is.

Now, the other interesting part of the story: When my parents decided to move to North Carolina, they had a very specific criteria list for the house they wanted to buy. Renting was not something that appealed to them. When my circumstances changed and I thought I was going to be moving, I offered them the idea that they could rent from me. Rich would still be close to work, and they would be close to all their doctors and everything. Once we called the wedding off, and I asked for my space, they were completely open to the idea of renting. And what a sweet thing for me to watch God do! And what an incredible blessing it is to have them so close to my house.

CHAPTER 49

Trafficked to Tell

"Naaman, commander of the army of the king of Syria, was a great man with his master and in high favor, because by him the LORD had given victory to Syria. He was a mighty man of valor, but he was a leper. Now the Syrians on one of their raids had carried off a little girl from the land of Israel, and she worked in the service of Naaman's wife. She said to her mistress, "Would that my lord were with the prophet who is in Samaria! He would cure him of his leprosy." So, Naaman went in and told his lord, "Thus and so spoke the girl from the land of Israel." And the king of Syria said, "Go now, and I will send a letter to the king of Israel."

—2 Kings 5:1-5 (ESV)

We sure do like to throw the phrase around, *"all things are possible with God,"* when things are going well or when a friend is in crisis, and we need something encouraging to say. But what about when we have no idea how our circumstances will turn out? When the sickness hasn't been cured, the relationship hasn't been healed, or the dream hasn't been fulfilled?

Often, I have found myself shaking my head at senseless tragedy or thinking nothing good could come from... fill in the blank with your example. What I find remarkable about the story of Naaman is how God reached him. *What's that you say?* Well, if you look closely at the story, you'll see the idea to go speak to Elisha came from a little girl. A little girl who served Naaman's wife, who had been carried off during a raid in Israel.

Did you catch that?

She was kidnapped. Stolen from her home and her parents were likely killed, perhaps even in front of her. And, this little girl tells her mistress that Naaman should go talk to the prophet to be healed! Can you imagine? Of course, we don't know how old she is or how long she has been in his home, but we know she has enough faith remaining to point her enemy captor to the king of Israel.

Ok, so just soak this in for a moment. In order to reach Naaman, God allowed one of His precious little girls to be abducted from her home so she may tell her mistress to have her husband talk to a prophet to be healed. This ... this is a mind-bending reality most Western believers like me cannot comprehend. God will do anything to reach His chosen, even allow calamity to fall upon His children so they will be put into positions where they can share the good news with people who don't know Jesus.

I don't know how it all plays out in God's economy, and how He can somehow cause good to come from terrible things, but I have seen it over and over again in my life, and maybe, just maybe, that hard spot that you're in right now, or the one you're about to be in … well, there's no maybe about it. God has orchestrated it, and if you'll allow yourself to stop and consider what He may be up to for His greater purpose, you may just find yourself giving thanks even when it looks like you shouldn't.

CHAPTER 50

Dodging Bullets

"Well as far as I'm concerned, it seems you've dodged a bullet."

—*Mary Crawley, Downton Abbey*

Shortly after Jesus made it abundantly clear I should not marry Jamison, I was binge watching Downton Abbey. In hindsight, it probably wasn't the best content for me to be consuming because the series takes place at a time in history when a woman's highest aim was to get married and make a name for herself. However, poor choices notwithstanding, as I was watching and enjoying all the characters and the fascinating interactions amongst them, I heard the gem of wisdom I needed right in that moment!

As Mary Crawley's cousin Claudette was heartbroken over a suitor turned cheater and losing the prospect of marriage one more time, Mary rightly categorizes the situation as dodging a bullet.

While the sudden loss of what I thought was going to be my future, I can only praise Jesus for answering my prayers to bring anything to light that needed to be seen. And, seen they were, and I thank Jesus every day for keeping me from making a bad decision and for giving me the wisdom to stop the whole thing.

Unlike the first time around the block, I had the experiential wisdom to see some patterns that would have presented significant challenges and I'm grateful Jesus put a stop to it and I listened.

CHAPTER 51

Well, That's Ridiculous

"'But, I never dreamed you would do anything like this! Lead me to an impassable precipice up which nothing can go but deer and goats, when I'm no more like a deer or a goat than is a jellyfish. It's too - it's too,' - Much Afraid fumbled for words, and then burst out laughing. 'Why, it's too preposterously absurd! It's crazy! Whatever will you do next?' The Shepard laughed too. 'I love doing preposterous things,' he replied. 'Why I don't know anything more exhilarating and delightful than turning weakness into strength, and fear into faith, and that which has been marred into perfection.'"

—Hinds Feet on High Places

I'd like to say my break-up was easy and clean, and we were able to resolve dividing property that was purchased to prepare for our future life without complications. Unfortunately, it dragged out for quite an unexpected time and required me to exercise my *"I'm not a doormat"* muscles. And, the whole thing only reinforced the very clear *"Do not marry him"* message.

The outcome, much to my consternation, meant I became the owner of a king-size mattress. To be clear, I didn't want it and was completely content with my XL twin, which was half of my previous king-size mattress. I had intended to purchase a queen-size mattress at some point, but I was definitely not in a rush. And, it wasn't MY plan. This just happened to me, or did it?

And, it wasn't just that I was getting a bigger bed, big whoop. It meant I had to rearrange furniture in three rooms. The chaos of the whole situation interrupted my peaceful refuge. I couldn't just be in my house and not think about almost getting married. It was as if my furniture was mocking me.

As I lay in my new obnoxiously large king-sized bed, I actually argued with Jesus about how silly it was for me to have this bed. And, how ridiculous it was for just me. And, as I argued, the Little Voice asked me if Jesus might know something I don't know. And, of course, I knew that He did.

I finally fell asleep, and the next morning, when I was spending time reading the Word and talking to Jesus about it, He reminded me how much He loves to do ridiculous things. Just like making

Much Afraid be able to go up an impassable precipice, He often does crazy things to get the glory.

Well, a couple days later, my dear friend Karen called. She and I have been friends since I was a junior in high school. She was my Young Life leader. At any rate, in a good year I usually get to see her and her family once. However, I had already seen her three times during the year, a rare treat. As it turns out, she and the boys would be in South Carolina for a soccer tournament, and she wanted to know if they could stay the night on their way back home. Well, as it turns out I now had not one, but two guest bedrooms and plenty of beds for my friends to sleep in.

And, well let's just say Jesus was kind to show me a little glimpse of what He was doing by giving me an obnoxiously large bed.

CHAPTER 52

From Loathing to Loving

"You turned my wailing into dancing; you removed my sackcloth and clothed me with joy."

—*Psalm 30:11 (NIV)*

Now, having my dear friends see my new home for the first time and being able to host them lessened the pain of the whole mattress ordeal of 2022. But, I couldn't shake the fact, the physical reminder of what that bed was supposed to be. While I was relieved I wasn't married to the specific man, the grief over broken dreams continued to flow.

I'm not sure where the idea started, but somewhere along the line, I decided I should make a headboard for my obnoxiously large bed. My bathroom and accompanying barn door both had a chevron theme, so I decided to go on Pinterest to see what inspiration I may be able to find. So, I started looking and lo and behold, I found exactly what I wanted.

The inspiration piece had a chevron headboard and footboard and had several different wood species. And, it just so turned out that Rich had kept a whole bunch of scrap wood from his old projects, and he somehow managed to get those into the Pod instead of my Mom's beloved garden pots. That's a whole other story.

With his scraps, I was able to make the headboard. And, well, I couldn't stop there. It really needed a footboard to complete the look. So, I tracked down a guy on Facebook Marketplace who sells rough-cut lumber. I ended up buying some more cherry, black walnut, red and white oak, and poplar.

And, well, it had all this space under the bed that was just wasted. So, I decided I should make drawers to make the most of it.

When it was all said and done, I ended up making a headboard, footboard and under bed drawers with a variety of cherry, red oak, white oak, cedar, pine, poplar and black walnut. And, now every time I look at my bed, I love it and think how wonderful a gift Jesus gave me in my obnoxiously large bed.

CHAPTER 53

Feeling A LOT Like Joseph

"The LORD was with Joseph, and he became a successful man, and he was in the house of his Egyptian master."

—*Genesis 39:2 (ESV)*

Over the years I have gained quite the fondness for the life of Joseph in the Bible. If you haven't read it, I highly recommend you do. His story begins in Genesis 37. His life is a picture of God working sovereignly behind the scenes to bring about His good plan for Israel and ultimately all of humanity. However, it doesn't go like you think it would go. It's not a straight shot. There is slavery. False accusations. Prison. Prosperity in the midst of pain. And, so much more.

Throughout the account of Joseph's life the phrase, "The LORD was with," or "because of Joseph, Potiphar was blessed," and so it goes over and over.

There are portions of his story where it seems God must have forgotten about him. He's in prison, and still in prison. But, then at just the right time, God raises up Joseph to help Pharaoh interpret some dreams and then just like that, Joseph is thrust into a position of power to save his family, his people and the rest of the world.

While I waited for God to deliver me from my broken marriage, I often languished and struggled to believe God hadn't forgotten about me. But, Joseph's story buoyed me. Despite feeling like I was stuck in a prison with my marriage and had no way out, I could point to God's movement in my life. I could see His faithfulness in my ministry and my work. I could see fruit and it gave me hope. It also reminded me we have no way of knowing what our God has in mind when things don't go the way we want. His plans are SO MUCH better than ours!

And, most recently I have been raised to a very important and powerful role within my company. I started as an admin nearly twenty years ago, and over the years the Lord has caused me to prosper and find favor with those I work with. While it is a secular business, I have been given the opportunity to make a tremendous impact for the good of my company and for the individuals I work with, and I can't help but thank God for His ways and thoughts that are higher than mine.

Because of the success the Lord has allowed me to have, I have a unique opportunity to share the hope I have with those who work with me. And who knows what plans God has for those I get to share the truth of the Gospel with? Maybe, just maybe, God may use one of these precious souls to do mighty deeds for His Kingdom and for the world.

CHAPTER 54

Best Author Ever

"Your eyes saw my unformed body; all the days ordained for me were written in your book before one of them came to be."

—*Psalm 139:16 (NIV)*

I am in a season of waiting. Waiting for the next thing. I don't know what the Lord has for me, so I've just been trying to live one day at a time and see how He wants me to use the abundance of time He has given me. As an unmarried woman who has no children, I sometimes have more time than I'd like.

On days when I have my head on straight and I intentionally remember Jesus is in control of everything, I enjoy the adventure and wonder of what each day may hold. It could be helping friends with a project, spending time with my parents, working on projects at my miracle home, or just being quiet and reading His Word.

But, other days. All that time can feel like a big void of "not doing anything." And, I have a tendency to measure my worth by what I'm doing or not doing.

I had dreams of having a family and doing ALL the things families do. Well, it would seem that– at least for now–that's not how my story goes. Or rather, I should say, *His story* for me goes. Speaking of stories, I often have very strong opinions about what my story should look like. When it doesn't go the way I think it should, it usually brings sadness and discontent. Thankfully, the Lord has given me His Word and other believers to help remind me who the greatest Author really is.

I'm a big fan of Sara Hagerty. She's written several books that have helped encourage me in my walk with Jesus. And, this past week, I was reading an email she sent out, and it essentially begged the question: if God would rather us read the story He is writing in our lives, or if we should be writing our own story, that inevitably will disappoint because He didn't write it.

As I wonder what's next, and battle grief shrapnel ... you know the random times when sadness over lost dreams strikes when you least expect it ... I take great comfort in the truth that THE KING of the UNIVERSE has written EVERY. SINGLE. DAY. in His book. He has an amazing story written for each one of us and we just need to partner with Him to see how it will turn out.

CHAPTER 55

I Am NOT Alone

"When you pass through the waters, I will be with you; and through the rivers, they shall not overwhelm you; when you walk through the fire you shall not be burned, and the flame shall not consume you."

—Isaiah 43:2 (ESV)

It's dawned on me that I've been struggling with loneliness. Living by myself and having a rather flexible schedule, aka my not-super-consistently-busy schedule, has put the spotlight on this emotion. As an extrovert who generally craves human interaction, I've noticed an increase in TV consumption on days when I don't get my people-interaction bucket filled. And, today, instead of turning on the TV to keep myself company, I asked Jesus why I wanted to watch TV so badly. His non-audible answer, "Because you're lonely, but I want you to write." So, I'm writing and reminding myself and you that we're NOT alone.

I decided to do a search on the Bible app to see how many times the phrase, "I will be with you" is mentioned. My first search pulled up that verse in Isaiah I used to open this little nugget, and then it also pulled up the one that inspired my wrist tattoo, "Fear not, *for I am with you*, be not dismayed for I am your God, I will strengthen you, I will help you, I will uphold you with my righteous right hand."

I had momentarily forgotten that part of the promise, "I am with you." I have **FEAR NOT** inked on my wrist to help me remember why I don't have to fear. But, my brain glossed over the "for I AM WITH YOU." I decided to dig a little more. Did you know eighty-three times the specific promise "I will be with you," was recorded in the Bible. That doesn't count the other gems like, I will never leave or forsake you, or I will carry you until your gray hair, or .... SO, many times it's repeated. I'm pretty sure it's repeated that many times because that's how much we need to be reminded that the God of the universe is with us. I know I do.

In previous seasons, this passage has resonated with me because of the deep waters and hot fire of living in near-constant trial, and not thinking it would ever end. It sustained me, knowing He was right there with me. And in this in-between season of learning how to live content with Jesus, the reminder that He is with me is just as powerful and needed.

I distinctly remember when I lived with Stephanie, my biggest fear in making the next step to buy my own house for just me was being alone. Being in my quiet house with no one to talk to, hang with, just be with... and you get the idea.

Most days, I would say I have adjusted to enjoying the refuge of a home Jesus has provided me. But, there are times when it's just a little too quiet for me. But, if I've learned anything, it's that Jesus knows when to send people into my life. And, ultimately, I am NEVER truly alone, and neither are you if you walk with Jesus and seek and look for Him intentionally.

CHAPTER 56

Who's Coming?

"Now, our God, we give you thanks, and praise your glorious name. But who am I, and who are my people, that we should be able to give as generously as this? Everything comes from you, and we have given you only what comes from your hand."

—*1 Chronicles 29:13-14 (NIV)*

Since Jesus made it abundantly clear to me to NOT marry Jamison, I have had a fair amount of time on my hands, and I've been having an ongoing conversation with Jesus about my house and who He wants to send to live in it. And, there has been an undeniable prompting to get my house ready for those who need refuge.

So, I've been focused on projects that will enable my home to be more useful or easier and more hospitable for those He may send.

At any rate, like He always does, He caused my friend Rachel to remember that I shared how God provided me my home and my desire is to use it to bless other people. And, it just so happens Rachel leads the women's ministry at my church and will have an intern working with her this summer. And, that intern needs housing. Now, she could have put Karly in an apartment, but Jesus prompted Rachel to ask if I'd consider hosting Karly this summer. As soon as she asked, I knew Jesus had orchestrated the whole thing.

How did I know?

Well, I would say in my almost thirty years of walking with Jesus, that He often warms my heart up to what He's going to do next. Like, I've been talking to Him and asking Him who He is going to send to my house.

Beyond that, I love women's ministry and particularly love encouraging younger women in the faith. The icing on the cake for me, beyond getting the blessing of being able to use the home Jesus gave me to bless someone else and pour into this young woman, I will have a roommate for three months!

CHAPTER 57

MmmKay Jesus

"Look among the nations, and see, wonder and be astounded. For I am doing a work in your days that you would not believe if told."

—Habakkuk 1:5 (ESV)

Have you ever been in a spot in life where things didn't go the way you expected, or were so far outside of what is considered typical that you were convinced it couldn't be good? Or the situation just looked so darn impossible, that you believed God couldn't do anything about it?

Well, Habakkuk had. In fact, over and over again in his authored book of the Bible he basically asks God all the questions we've asked. *Where are you God? How long is this going to last?* It's a raw account with real emotions and hard questions, and God answers him. I LOVE THIS. God answers his hard questions and it's documented. That means we can take our tough questions to Jesus.

Now, how God answers Habakkuk caught my attention. God basically says, *"I'm going to do something amazing, and you wouldn't believe me if I told you."*

Why that caught my attention, in this season, I have a tendency to believe that the ultimate human experience would be to be married and be a mom. It's what I've always desired for as long as I can remember. But, that is NOT what Jesus has written for my story. As I write this, I realize I've covered facets of this wrestling in earlier chapters, yet the lesson Jesus has been showing me is slightly different than I've shared before.

The question that came to mind after reading this passage, while about a completely different set of circumstances, God sharing how He would raise up an enemy army to discipline His people, for me it translated to ... *what if you can't imagine that I have something immeasurably more fulfilling and astounding than being married and being a biological mom?*

If THE GOD OF THE UNIVERSE wrote my story, and I believe He is GOOD and He writes perfect stories, then my only conclusion can be that yes, He does have something EVEN more amazing planned for me, that if He told me I would NOT believe. Same goes for you, if you know Him.

CHAPTER 58

Even if...

"Though the fig tree should not blossom, nor fruit be on the vines, the produce of the olive fail and the fields yield no food, the flock be cut off from the fold and there be no herd in the stalls, YET [emphasis mine] I will rejoice in the Lord. I will take joy in the God of my salvation. God, the Lord, is my strength; he makes my feet like the deer's; he makes me tread on my high places."

—Habakkuk 3:17-19 (ESV)

Back-to-back mentions from Hab-a-who? If you haven't read Habakkuk, you should. It's in the Old Testament and has so many treasures in it. For this one, following all of Habakkuk's questions to God about what in the world is going on, we see a huge shift.

A shift to choose to rejoice when the worst of the worst is going on in his world. He and all of Israel, starving, no hope of having any income or relief from their pain, and he declares YET he will rejoice.

What's your "even if," that has you questioning God's care, concern or goodness? If I were to fill in those blanks, it would likely sound something like, *"Though I've been divorced and have no prospects of getting married; though I am not being embraced by a man and will likely never have biological children and may be pitied by my friends and family, yet I will rejoice in the Lord."*

We can take joy in the God of our salvation even during the most painful times. He IS our strength. He makes us thrive on the heights. He does it.

Along with laying down my desires, dreams, hopes and my vision for what my perfect story should be, Jesus has just been so faithful to bring scripture to mind that I've read years ago to address my current reality.

As I have been intentionally leaning in to surrender to the story Jesus has written for my life, He brought a sweet promise to mind from Isaiah 46:3-4 (ESV). It says, *"Listen to me, O house of Jacob, all the remnant of the house of Israel, who have been borne by me from before birth carried from the womb; even to your old age I am he, and to your gray hairs I will carry you. I have made, and I will bear; I will carry and will save."*

What an astounding promise! Even to my gray hairs God will carry me. The One who made us, drew up plans for our lives will NOT abandon us, EVER. Our God who brought us into existence will NOT leave us as orphans and that is reason enough to rejoice.

Tending Sheep
- PITA

"Simon, son of John, do you love me more than these?" He said to him, "Yes, Lord; You know that I love you." He said, "Feed my lambs." He said to him a second time, "Simon, son of John, do you love me?" He said, "Yes, Lord; You know that I love you." He said to him, "Tend my sheep." He said to him a third time. "Simon, son of John, do you love me?" Peter was grieved because he said to him the third time, "Do you love me?" and he said to him, "Lord, you know everything, you know that I love you." Jesus said to him, "Feed my sheep."

—John 21:15-18 (ESV)

Recently, God has been showing me just how big an honor it is for Him to call us to care for or tend His sheep. Sure, shepherding sheep can be smelly, messy and tiring work, but not everyone gets to play the role of caregiver to sheep. While you may have thought PITA stood for something else, e'hem, I think we need to reframe it as Privilege In The Assignment.

Full disclosure, sometimes I don't want to tend the sheep. Sometimes I think I'm a better sheep than the rest. Sometimes the sheep Jesus has called me to care for aren't the ones I would pick. My criteria, if I'm honest, would be more aligned to my personal preferences. The ones who meet MY needs.

But, the thing about tending and caring for sheep, Jesus calls us to do it, and it's a sign of belonging to Him. And, it's a reminder to us, to me really, that we're all messy, needy, and less-than-smart sheep.

Jesus hasn't looked at my messy heart and said, *"No you're too much and I can't handle the inconvenience of caring for you."* He also hasn't said, *"I have other things on my agenda today, so I don't have time for you. Or I don't really like you, so I think I'll avoid you."* Ouch.

So, the encouragement is to remember He only entrusts His sheep to those who love Him and those He wants to know in a deeper, more intimate way.

CHAPTER 60

Jesus So Tolerated

"We who are strong have an obligation to bear with the failings of the weak, and not to please ourselves. Let each of us please his neighbor for his good, to build him up. For Christ did not please himself, but as it is written, "The reproaches of those who reproached you fell on me." For whatever was written in former days was written for our instruction, that through endurance and through the encouragement of the Scriptures we might have hope. May the God of endurance and encouragement grant you to live in such harmony with one another, in accord with Christ Jesus, that together you may with one voice glorify the God and Father of our Lord Jesus Christ. Therefore welcome one another as Christ has welcomed you, for the glory of God."

—Romans 15:1-7 (ESV)

This summer, I decided to sign up for my church's summer women's Bible study on the book of Galatians. Completely unlike any other study I've ever done, this one didn't have a set group of questions. It invited attendees to read, ask questions and discuss. At first, my resistant heart didn't appreciate the foreign format. It wasn't my preference and, well, it didn't have the same relational component I had become accustomed to enjoying with all the studies I had ever done.

Confession, I even bailed on a week when I decided it *just wasn't for me.* Then Jesus did something. He convicted my heart about my need to be there for my ladies, and I had a need to be there to be a part of what He wanted to do *in me.*

The last night, as we talked about chapter 6:2 it said, *"Bear one another's burdens, and so fulfill the law of Christ."* And, we had several different thoughts on what that might mean. But the word "bear" stood out to me, so I did some cross referencing and landed in Romans 15. The alternate meaning for bear in the verse above is "tolerate." And, then I dug further and the Little Voice was like I don't just "tolerate" my kids, I love them.

And, that is the exact moment my heart was convicted of showing preference to people who I just genuinely enjoy and who get me. They may have a mess, but it's not a full-out trainwreck or it may be a trainwreck, but in and of themselves they're not trainwrecks. But, there are some people in my life who ... well, are just really broken, and Jesus sought those people out. Whether they were the completely conceited Pharisees, the lame, the outcasts … ALL the people. Jesus cared and intentionally invited them in to be with Him. Heck, Jesus sought me out when my life and heart were one big trainwreck, and there were people He put in my life who cared for me on His behalf.

Oh, that we would repent from thinking we're better than we are and welcome those who take more Jesus in us to love them. *Ahhhhhh, that's the thing right?!?* Jesus wants more of Him in us and one of the ways He gets more of Him in us is when we have to rely on Him for His strength to do the things we CANNOT do in our own strength.

CHAPTER 61

Hesed Adventure

"Therefore, behold, I will allure her, and bring her into the wilderness, and speak tenderly to her. And there I will give her her vineyards and make the Valley of Achor a door of hope. And there she shall answer as in the days of her youth, as at the time when she came out of the land of Egypt."

—Hosea 2:14-15 (ESV)

It's almost been a year since I broke my engagement off, and I'm OK with that, though I would be lying if I said I didn't get lonely more often than I'd like. In fact, for the past several months, Jesus has orchestrated my schedule in such a way that I have had WAY more time on my hands than I would like. I wrote about it already; geeze, there's a theme here.

At any rate, because I didn't go on a honeymoon, I have had a flight credit sitting there, needing to be used, and for months I let it sit there because the prospect of going on a trip by myself did NOT in any WAY sound fun. I'm the quintessential people-person. And, Jesus has just been like, *"I want to take you away on a trip, just you and me."* And, I've been like, *"But that doesn't sound fun."*

I half-heartedly looked into hiking destinations over the months, because I just reread "Hind's Feet on High Places." It takes place in Switzerland, in the Alps, and I was like, *"Yeah, I should go there,"* but then it was a little more spendy than I was ready to commit to, so closed door on that one.

Anyway, fast forward like six weeks ago, when it was crazy hot outside and I knew I couldn't do any yard work or any other outdoor adventure without instantaneously combusting, the Little Voice was like, "You need to investigate your flight credit." So, I did. Well, it was over $600 and needed to be used by August 7th! Whoa, buddy! So, I spent the next couple of hours googling the best hiking in the U.S. in August, and Washington state, Mt. Rainier was at the top of the list. And, my flight credit covered most of the fare.

So, I'm currently sitting in the rocking chairs at the Charlotte airport, waiting for my flight that is delayed, and praying I still get out tonight. The beauty in my "delay" is it gave me a chance to sit here and add some more bits in this collection of things Jesus has inspired me to capture and share.

What He's impressed on my heart through a book I've started to listen to from Ann Voskamp, "Waymaker," is that He is the only one who has Hesed love, or loyal love for me. Not my best friend, or a husband, parent, anyone... no one can love me like Jesus does. And He is SO SO SO very excited to go on this adventure with me. And, He wants to go on ALL the adventures with You, too!

He made the places I'm going to see and knows all the nooks and crannies. And He has incredible things planned for our time together. I can't wait to share what He does!

CHAPTER 62

Slowcooker Sanctification

"Being confident of this, that he who began a good work in you will carry it to completion."

—*Philippians 1:6 (NIV)*

I love a good crockpot recipe. You take all the ingredients, put 'em in the pot, turn on the thing, come back four, six, ten hours later, and you have a tasty meal. The effort involved is usually minimal, and you have leftovers for days! I love some leftovers. But, you can't speed it up, and lifting the lid in the middle can mess with how long it takes to cook your meal.

But, what has me thinking about crockpots right now, you ask? Well, on this adventure I'm having in the PNW (Pacific Northwest) with Jesus, the Little Voice prompted me to bring the book, "Unseen," by Sara Hagerty with me. It's been sitting on my nightstand since sometime in 2021, partially read, and I got distracted with reading other things until right now.

Well, it turns out the book's message is all about the incredible work God does in our hearts when we lean into the moments to be with Him when no one else can see. Hmm, sounds vaguely familiar, ummm, like a trip to the PNW where no one else but Jesus has a view of the happenings of this trip, outside of those I'm texting with. I'm still off of social media and I don't regret it for one single moment.

At any rate, today was full-on day two of my adventure. I went to bed at 6:30 PM PST because I was dead tired after the delay and didn't get to bed until like 2 AM. Unfortunately, it was raining when I woke up. Whomp, whomp. Like, I had ideas of wanting to go to crazy cool places today. I had some adventure to find, something tangible to say I got my money's worth from this adventure.

And, the Little Voice was like, *"I brought the rain so you could be still with me today."* He forced me, in a very gentle-rain-kind-of-way to be with Him, with no agenda and no itinerary. And, I just "so happen" to have the book that I pressed pause on to help my heart that wasn't ready for being unseen in 2021 to try again in 2023.

Oh, the kindness of Jesus to not force sanctification on us. He understands our weaknesses, and knows when we will be receptive to His nudges.

So, I ended up spending half a day reading, talking to Jesus, and trying to be still. And I don't have one single photo to document how "amazing" my day was. However, I do have one photo of me from after my impromptu adventure to what was supposed to be an amazing waterfall. The photo documented my fall into the creek, which resembled me wetting myself, after I attempted to jump onto a slippery rock and ended up with a bruised knee and a wet backside. I'm not sure if the takeaway was "you should have stayed still" or if it was something else altogether, but many times the most valuable moments can't be documented, or aren't meant to be, outside of our knowing-Savior's view. That, I'm learning, has more value than the most amazing view or adventure.

CHAPTER 63

Efficiency Isn't Everything

"Now as they went on their way, Jesus entered a village. And a woman named Martha welcomed him into her house. And she had a sister called Mary, who sat at the Lord's feet and listened to his teaching. But Martha was distracted with much serving. And she went up to him and said, "Lord, do you not care that my sister has left me to serve alone? Tell her then to help me." But the Lord answered her, "Martha, Martha you are anxious and troubled about many things, but one thing is necessary. Mary has chosen the good portion, which will not be taken away from her."

—Luke 10:38-42 (ESV)

I'm quite familiar with the story of Martha and Mary. Mary sits and listens to Jesus; she is still. Martha is the go-getter and has an agenda for her day.

On this PNW adventure, I found myself anxious about whether I was going to see and do everything I needed to in order for this trip to be "worth it." And moreover, would my friends and family, or my human onlookers, think I had spent my time and money well? Ugh.

In that ongoing theme of being still, like Mary in this story, Jesus impressed on me how my day-to-day drive for efficiency is a huge part of my nine-to-five gig, and also a central part of our Western culture. How much did I cram into my day? Did I see "enough," do "enough"? Or did I waste it? *Did I miss out on something?*

In reading "Unseen," and taking time to slow down and be still and really try to listen to what Jesus may be saying to my heart, similar to what I read from Sara, the phrase "immeasurable purpose" came to mind.

Rather than be anxious, as I spent half a day indoors and not doing "anything," Jesus was like, *"I've got your itinerary planned, and you're not going to miss one thing you're supposed to do/see. You let me worry about what and where we'll go."*

So, I laid down my ideas of what I "should" see and do on Saturday morning. The forecast did not look great for seeing Mt. Rainier, and well, I wasn't quite sure where Jesus wanted to go.

What I encountered, well let's just say Jesus is a much better travel agent than I am. And beyond this trip, He knows ALL of our days and EVERY moment of EVERY day. If we lived like we believed that He cared about all the minutiae of traffic, interruptions, and things going NOT the way we want, and considered perhaps He has something else on His agenda for us, we may be able to lay down our idol of efficiency and behold His care for us in ways we've never experienced before.

CHAPTER 64

Trusting the BEST
Travel Agent

"The Lord will fulfill his purpose for me; your steadfast love, O Lord, endures forever. Do not forsake the work of your hands."

—Psalm 138:8 (NIV)

I had ideas about what I should see during my trip to Mt. Rainier. Mainly Mt. Rainier, waterfalls, and wildflowers. Those three things were on my bucket list. And with park traffic being crazy on the weekends and rain and clouds regularly hiding the mountain, part of me had my doubts about whether I'd really get to see my wish list.

The result? I had to fight to trust. I had to use the truth of His Word to calm my anxious heart. If Jesus has indeed written every single day, which He has, and if He has made every single thing in creation, then He certainly knows all the nooks and crannies of Mt. Rainier and the surrounding area, and I can trust Him to order my day according to what He wants me to experience.

Sunday morning I woke up to *more* rain.

Whomp, whomp. Worry about a wasted trip tried to overtake me, then the LV nudged me to read Psalm 46.

The part He brought to mind was, *"Cease striving and know that I'm God"* (Psalm 46:10 NASB).

So, I cracked my Bible open to Psalm 46 and spent some time reading, journaling, and being still with Jesus.

God is our refuge and strength,
 a very present help in trouble.
Therefore we will not fear though the earth gives way,
  though the mountains be moved into the heart of the sea,
though its waters roar and foam,
  though the mountains tremble at its swelling. Selah
There is a river whose streams make glad the city of God,
  the holy habitation of the Most High.
God is in the midst of her; she shall not be moved;
  God will help her when morning dawns.
The nations rage, the kingdoms totter;
  he utters his voice, the earth melts.
The Lord of hosts is with us;
  the God of Jacob is our fortress. Selah

Come, behold the works of the Lord,
  how he has brought desolations on the earth.
He makes wars cease to the end of the earth;
  he breaks the bow and shatters the spear;
  he burns the chariots with fire.
"Be still, and know that I am God.
  I will be exalted among the nations,
  I will be exalted in the earth!"
The Lord of hosts is with us;
  the God of Jacob is our fortress.

After reading it, I simply asked Him what He wanted me to see.

Naturally, I went on to one of the blogger's sites I had previously checked out and started to relook at the fifteen must-do hikes blog I had already read. As I was reading, I came across a bit about Silver Falls in the southern part of Mt. Rainier, Ohanapecosh.

And the call outs, *"great for cloudy/rainy days and not a hot spot of the park."*

Ahhhh, ok, so it seemed like a good plan, and I wanted to take the gondola up in Crystal Valley, an adjacent ski resort, and see if I might catch a glimpse of the mountain, despite the cloudy weather. I punched both into my phone GPS and set out on my way.

Oh my, Silver Falls—words cannot describe how glorious. Besides having an incredible aqua/teal color to the water, it was absolutely crystal clear. You could see all the way to the bottom of the river.

And then I remembered what Jesus had me read earlier in Psalm 46.

"There is a river whose streams make glad the city of God,

the holy habitation of the Most High.

God is in the midst of her; she shall not be moved;

God will help her when morning dawns."

The water I had in front of me reminded me of the heavenly picture I read about only about hours before. And my heart leapt, thinking about how Jesus orchestrated me seeing this incredible glimpse of what the stream in the city of God may look like, and then dually promised that His city and I wouldn't be moved, and He would help me when the morning dawns.

As I reflected on the passage, it made me think of another passage about heavenly rivers.

"Then the angel showed me the river of the water of life, bright as crystal, flowing from the throne of God and the Lamb..."

—Revelation 22:1 (ESV)

After finishing my lunch, which I ate by the river bank with an amazing view, it seemed good to go ahead and give the gondola ride a shot. The skies had cleared up a bit and maybe, just maybe, I might be able to see the mountain. But, no cell service and I didn't remember the route from looking it up. Soooo, I just decided to drive and see if I couldn't figure it out. From Ohanapecosh, I headed toward White Pass, and lo and behold, I had all the bars. And, I figured out that I had to go exactly back the way I came and then a bit further. So, I'd basically gone twenty miles "out of my way."

Now, this is just ONE cool surprise Jesus planned. As I drove back to get to Crystal Valley, the clouds disappeared and right smack-dab in the middle of my view was Mt. Rainier. He had me go "out of my way" and be "inefficient" so I could catch a glimpse of the mammoth beauty.

After the gondola ride and experiencing a view like no other of the mountain, I remembered that the local hikers I ran into on Friday afternoon had recommended Sunrise. With it being late in the day, I figured it couldn't hurt to try. Oh my, Jesus took away ALL the clouds and I got to see the mountain in ALL of its beauty. A rarity if you've not visited the area.

I had to pick my jaw up off the ground after seeing so many incredible things. But Jesus had me go see Silver Falls first. And relative to Sunrise, the wildflowers were already mostly petered out, so that left me a little meh, but where I landed, Jesus knows my love language is waterfalls and He let me see that one first in His itinerary for this trip. I'm smitten and so very grateful.

He also knows I love surprises, and I couldn't have been more surprised. Oh, how He loves to give good gifts to ALL His beloved children.

CHAPTER 65

The Creation Praise Chorus

"You will go out in joy and be led forth in peace; the mountains and hills will burst into song before you, and all the trees of the field will clap their hands."

—*Isaiah 55:12 (NIV)*

I spent A LOT of time in the car driving to all the gloriously beautiful places Jesus made just for me. And while I was exploring, the verse about trees clapping their hands came to mind. All along many of the roads in Washington, and especially in the national parks, as far as the eye can see it's green. On the mountains, throngs and throngs of fir, redwood, cedar and grow and all look like they're giving a standing ovation to the King.

But, beyond the view from behind the steering wheel, EVERY. SINGLE. THING I saw pointed to THE Creator. The One and Only who made moss to grow on trees and boulders beside streams, and who planted wildflower after wildflower in glorious splendor.

The last day of my trip, Jesus put the chef's kiss on His itinerary for my trip. Paradise, yeah, part of Mt. Rainier holds that distinction. And, it lived up to its name in every way.

My bucket list: waterfalls and wildflowers. I had Comet Falls on my radar. But, literally, each moment I kept talking and listening to Jesus about what He had in mind for our itinerary.

I initially thought I'd tackle Comet Falls first, but sensed I should head to the Paradise visitor center. Despite following the local hikers' advice and waiting until Monday to go, the parking lot still overflowed. As I drove past the visitor center, and started down the mountain, Jesus provided a parking spot and the perfect place to eat my lunch, on the embankment of the Paradise river and falls.

Yes, *I had lunch in Paradise,* where a series of mini falls, wildflowers and a friendly marmot made me giddy.

While I thought it would be nice to see the mountain again, I had seen it the day before, so any sighting this day would just be the proverbial "cherry on top" of my trip. And, my hopes were not high as every hiker confirmed *"the mount'in's not out."*

As I explored the area, a trailhead only a stone's throw away led to a path along the waterfall and connected to the famous Skyline Trail, a trail I had hoped to trek. That trail led through a sea of wildflowers, led me to famous Myrtle Falls, and just as I rounded a turn on the trail, Jesus gave me a glimpse of the mountain with a brief break in the clouds. Oh, so brief a view, but again another sweet gift for my last day.

Literally, everything everyone said about the wildflowers ...100% true. Such a stunning show, and my heart felt completely full from all the beauty Jesus prepared for me.

Then for His Grand Finale of surprises ... Comet Falls Trail.

This one needs its very own diddy.

CHAPTER 66

Worth Every Single Step

"Therefore since we are surrounded by such a great cloud of witnesses, let us also lay aside every weight, and sin which clings so closely, and let us run with endurance the race that is set before us, looking to Jesus the author and perfecter of our faith, who for the joy that was set before Him endured the cross, despising the shame, and is seated at the right hand of God."

—Hebrews 12:1-2 (ESV)

The Van Trump Trail which leads to Comet Falls is 3.8 miles round trip with an elevation change of 900 feet.

That doesn't sound like that much. Totally doable, right?

Well, after having already put in about four miles earlier in the day I thought, *"I can do this. And, c'mon it's the last thing you're going to see on this trip."*

Shortly into the hike I passed a couple guys and, of course, asked them if it was worth it. I needed to know if I could and should commit to adding another four miles to my step count for the day. They gave a solid affirmation of my continuation, but did say, *"Well we didn't go all the way to the top, but it was good."*

That seemed to be a satisfactory answer to me, and after all, a waterfall awaited my enjoyment. The very first bridge... maybe fifteen minutes into the hike, and *oh my goodness,* the roar, the multiple-level falls, the mossy rocks, my eyes could hardly contain my joy.

So, I continued on my trek. The river on my left and every ten minutes or so, another mini waterfall, and another, and another. And then, the trail turned a bit, and while I could still hear the water, I couldn't see it anymore. And the incline became greater, and my lack of snack packing and extra water began to come to the forefront of my brain.

Then just when I needed it, a couple of young ladies who had already been to the top and soaked in the glory, came my way. Of course, I had to ask, *"Was it worth it?"* And they both gave a hearty yes! And then they said something different than the first group. *"Oh, but don't stop at the bottom, you have to actually go up and feel the waterfall on you!"* With that endorsement, I had to keep going.

Then, after ascending what seemed to be a never-ending stone-made staircase, in the sun and weary from the climb, Jesus sent another group of cheerleaders. They were a few decades older than me and exclaimed the same encouragement.

And, when I turned the corner past the sign that said, "Comet Falls 200 feet," I literally laughed out loud with delight over the splendor and majesty of falls pouring over the edge in sheer abandon. I sat for a few moments to take it in, then took the extra ten minutes to get close enough to let the falls "get on me." Such a remarkable experience and completely worth every step up and every step back down the trail.

In hindsight, I'm not sure I would have kept going without the words of encouragement I heard along the way. They played a tremendous role in me persevering to reach the summit. Several times I thought, it can't be that great, but the words of those who had gone before me helped me to press on to experience ALL of the wonder.

I could have stopped short and still enjoyed it, but going the distance was 1,000% worth it.

And, likewise on my way down I ran into a couple of groups of ladies and encouraged them the same way, *"It's soooo worth it!"*

Same goes for the Christian life. So often we don't think it's worth it because it's hard and the end seems so far away. But we can know it is worth it, and can keep trekking and encourage others to do the same. And not only that, but the joy we experience now can be correlated to how much we decide to be all in.

Half-hearted trekking doesn't produce nearly the delight as pouring yourself out completely.

And I'd be remiss if I failed to point out the omniscience of Jesus to know what would thrill me the most and orchestrate my day, and the whole trip for that matter, in such a way as to save the very best for last.

CHAPTER 67

A Case of the Supposed-tos

"Then Job replied to the Lord: I know that you can do all things; no purpose of yours can be thwarted."

—Job 42:1-2 (NIV)

Upon returning from my grand solo adventure with Jesus, this terrible thing happened.

I had an irrational dread of being alone.

I mean, seriously, I just spent five and a half days with just Jesus in bliss and not wanting to come back, and yet in Raleigh in my house ...

I didn't feel ok being alone.

Naturally, I wondered what in the world that could be about. So, I asked Jesus to show me what wrong thought, or thoughts were under the surface and creating such anxiety for me.

Turns out, He showed me I had a case of the "supposed-tos." As in, at the very core of my being I was believing the lie that me being in my house, by myself, not married and alone at forty-six is not what my story is supposed to be. So, what's the harm in letting that narrative play in our brains?

That narrative has several wrong conclusions tied to it.

God doesn't know what He's doing.

My life and circumstances are haphazard, and God is NOT in control.

God doesn't love me; if He did, He would have done ... fill in the blank.

I repented of allowing those thoughts to be in my mind, and asked for forgiveness for believing the lies associated with them. And, my angst disappeared, at least until I let those thoughts sneak back in again.

Hopefully, I'll remember Job who had a very severe case of the "supposed-tos." In all honesty, I completely get why Job had his case.

Literally, EVERY single blessing in his life was removed. And he decided he knew better than the God of the universe. Well, let's just say, God put Job in his place.

Even in the worst of heartbreaks, God has a loving purpose, and our little human dust brains cannot comprehend what He knows. In those moments, we have to lean in and trust that He is good, and everything He does is good.

CHAPTER 68

Look at Me!

"Whatever you do, work at it with all your heart, as working for the Lord, and not for man."

—*Colossians 3:23 (NIV)*

R ecently, I offered to watch my friend's dog, Cooper, a black lab who has hunting and all the ball fetching in his DNA. I've known Cooper since he was just a pup and have been one of his people since the first time we met. While Cooper can be fully conked out on his bed, as soon as he hears my voice or knows I've set foot in his house, he goes just a bit bananas.

He used to live next door to me, but my friends and I have moved from our old neighborhood and now if I watch Cooper for them, they bring him to me because I'm a sleep diva and really love my bed, my house, and well, enough said.

When Cooper comes to stay with me, he has a very large yard to play in, which just so happens to include a giant hard red plastic ball—like 1.5 feet in diameter.

And, since he discovered the giant red ball, he lives to play with it when he comes to my house. His whole priority list changes. While playing typically lands near the top of the list, food usually takes the number one spot. But I would even go so far as to say Cooper is obsessed with the giant red ball.

Now, that's not all that interesting, but what brought Cooper and the giant red ball to mind is how he will only really play all out with the ball—pushing it around the yard and barking like a maniac for an extended amount of time—if I'm watching him do it. And if I dare go back in the house to take care of my to-do list he stops and sits in the yard and barks until I come back outside. It's as if he wants to say, *"Hey, look at me! Look what I'm doing!"*

And, while I'm not Cooper, I often want an audience or acknowledgment of whatever I've done to affirm my worth, like Cooper does. And, I would argue we've been designed to want to please those we love. But, when I perform for anyone but Jesus, I usually end up figuratively sitting down and barking until they come back. The outcome, as you would imagine, leaves a lot to be desired. Beyond being annoying and, well, annoying, people have other things to do besides praise us for what we've accomplished.

And waiting around for man's applause can mean we waste the time we've been given.

But if we seek the applause of the One and Only King of the universe, we can do whatever He has called us to do with all of our might and know He sees every single moment. He doesn't get worn out by our asking Him to watch, and we actually don't have to ask Him to watch because He sees us all the time. And the other benefit? His pleasure in us doesn't depend on our performance. He delights in us whether we push our giant red ball around with gusto or not.

CHAPTER 69

BFFs With Jesus

"A man of many companions may come to ruin, but there is a friend who sticks closer than a brother."

—*Proverbs 18:24 (ESV)*

Have you ever had the experience of meeting someone and deciding you wanted to be friends with them? Maybe the conversation was great, or their sense of humor and way of relating just clicked with you, or perhaps they just made you feel welcomed and wanted? Well, if you're anything like me, you've likely had that experience multiple times in your life.

I've also noticed something else as I've gotten older and have friends in different seasons of life: sometimes, for whatever reason, not all friendships remain intact or as close as they were when they began.

As a human who genuinely loves being around people, and for all intents and purposes is a recovering people pleaser, I used to take those shifts in friendship personally. Because I used to equate my worth with being able to sustain and maintain strong friendships with everyone all the time, I would be crushed when the relationship changed. And frequently I would wonder what I had done to cause the relationship to change.

But Jesus has been showing me some things about friendship over the last several years. Because I have a tendency to put too much hope in my friendships and make them into idols, I've noticed Jesus really wants me to hold all of my friendships loosely. For me, I have to continually check my heart to see if I'm unintentionally putting too much on any one friend, or essentially looking for them to be what only Jesus can be for me.

Being in a somewhat odd season of life that doesn't match most of my peers, I have longed to have one friend who has a similar story and similar amount of time on her hands so I could have more consistent companionship. And even a dear friend of mine prayed Jesus would provide such a friend.

And you know what He whispered to me?

"I'm that friend you're looking for and I'm inviting you into the deepest, sweetest, most satisfying friendship you've ever experienced."

Perhaps you've recently had a friendship dissolve for one reason or another, and you're crushed about it. I wonder if that dissolving wasn't at least in part so you could have the opportunity to go deeper with Jesus and encounter Him as your BFF?

I'm beyond sure that's part of the purpose of this particular season for me. Will you accept His invitation?

CHAPTER 70

Unconventional Motherhood

"'Sing, O barren one, who did not bear; break forth into singing and cry aloud, you who have not been in labor! For the children of the desolate one will be more than the children of her who is married,' says the Lord."

—*Isaiah 54:1 (ESV)*

More and more, I find myself not really fitting into "a nice and clean demographic." I'm forty-seven, divorced after eighteen plus years, and I have no children. And you're like, "Yeah, you've mentioned that a time or two in your book." Well, maybe you're not, and that's just the narrative in my head, but it's a thing.

It's still a thing.

And, to be perfectly honest, I don't know if it will ever not be a thing. I share that simply to state the obvious: that not being a mom, at times, can still be a very hard and painful thing. And, my guess ... that feeling and battle may be part of your journey or part of someone else's journey you know.

Now don't get me wrong, there have also been plenty of times over the years that I have praised Jesus because I'm not a mom. I see you and how hard it is. And, I don't even know half of it, no doubt.

On a more humorous note, yes, I should most definitely sing because I haven't experienced morning sickness, torn lady parts and sleepless nights.

But seriously, it's hard when our life dreams don't match up to what Jesus has written in our stories.

I can remember times when Mother's Day would roll around, and I would just want to curl up into the fetal position and cry all day. A friend would text and tell me how I've helped her and others grow in their faith, or the season when I volunteered in the preschool ministry and got to teach those littles about Jesus. For that season, I had the privilege of being a spiritual parent, and the kind words parents would bestow on me for volunteering my time ... I could see glimpses of the promise above coming to fruition in my life.

This promise God gives us in the book of Isaiah has brought much comfort to me over the years as I think about the prospect that Jesus may not have biological motherhood in my storyline.

I love to sing. I mean, I REALLY love to sing. Now I know I'm no Carrie Underwood or Lauren Daigle, but my heart leaps when I get to sing. And I love that God tells the barren woman who hasn't born a single child to break forth into singing because she will have more children than she who is married. Unlike my joke above, the motivation for our singing won't be because of the pain we have avoided, no it's much sweeter than that.

Now how can that be, you say?

Is He talking about adoption and opening up an orphanage?

No, I believe this promise relates directly to the ability of any woman to be a spiritual mother to younger believers in Christ. And, if you happen to be a man with similar desires to be a dad, I believe the promise applies to those dreams too. Similar to the way Paul saw Timothy as a son in the faith, as mature believers we can pour into the Body of Christ and watch Jesus multiply our spiritual offspring beyond anything we can comprehend. I imagine when we get to heaven we'll be quite shocked to see how Jesus has fulfilled this promise for each of us who know Him.

CHAPTER 71

Cows in Spandex

"Everyone then who hears these words of mine and does them will be like a wise man who built his house on the rock. And the rain fell, and the floods came, and the winds blew and beat on that house, but it did not fall, because it had been founded on the rock. And everyone who hears these words of mine and does not do them will be like a foolish man who built his house on the sand. And the rain fell, and the floods came, and the winds blew and beat against that house, and it fell, and great was the fall of it."

—Matthew 7:24-26 (ESV)

I recently needed to go to the doctor for a minor issue, and per the usual routine, they put me on the scale. However, unlike every other time I've been to the doctor in, well, probably my whole life, I made the tragic mistake of looking down at the scale when the unfathomable number appeared on the screen.

One, mind you, I had never anticipated seeing in my lifetime, and one that was **twenty pounds more** than the figure that had been recorded a mere eight months prior.

I loudly exclaimed, *"I'm a cow!"*

The technician quickly piped up to scold me for saying such a thing and then proceeded to tell me I looked fabulous. Well, fabulous or not, that number was not a healthy one, and one which had me wondering if something serious may be wrong with my health.

I mean, had I really eaten twenty pounds worth of tortilla chips over the past eight months? Sure, I had been lifting weights once a week since about the same time, but that wouldn't put on that much muscle, and my frame certainly didn't indicate that as the source. After getting an exceptionally clean bill of health according to my regular blood panel, I decided I needed to take the plunge and sign up for one of those apps to help me be more mindful about my eating.

But, I've been thinking, how did I get here?

I don't own a scale and haven't had one for years because there was a time when I was obsessed with my weight. But living in a post-pandemic world with A LOT of spandex has given me an inaccurate view of my level of fitness. I mean I still fit into my tights and most of my pants. Sure, a few of them seem to not want to button around my middle, but c'mon, the stretchy ones work.

And then it made me think about how being stretchy or not well-defined with the truth of God's Word can lead to all kinds of mishaps in life. Or another way of saying it, standing on shifting sand. My experience with my spandex led me to believe I had only gained a little bit of weight around my middle. But in actuality, I have actually packed on several pounds all over my body. The tape measure confirmed that today. When we don't have a concrete understanding of God's Truth, it can lead to all kinds of wrong beliefs and unnecessary pain.

So, while I won't be giving up my spandex anytime soon, I will be investing in a scale and not letting my stretchy pants be the guide of my health, but will rely on the concrete standards of reality that show up on the little rectangle on the floor. And I'll continue to use God's Word as my plumb line or my Rock, not some shifting, inconsistent measure like my feelings.

CHAPTER 72

You're Asking The Wrong Question

"Every good gift and every perfect gift is from above, and comes down from the Father of lights, with whom there is no variation or shadow of turning."

—*James 1:17 (NIV)*

In advance of my birthday this year, a dear friend asked me how I would define a "good birthday." Deep question, as I inched closer to beginning my forty-seventh lap around the sun. I had been talking to Jesus about that very thing though before she asked the question.

Would "good" be ... dinner with my parents, friends taking me out, a big party, a month-long string of events, texts, coffees, meals, and trips ... I wasn't exactly sure how I would define a "good birthday." I'm not sure when the LV nudged me, but what seemed to be crystal clear to me, Jesus knew what I needed for my birthday, and I wanted to welcome whatever He deemed to be good for this year's celebration.

Now for the backstory on this one because it has been decades in the making. I'm not certain of the year, but a song entitled "Good, Good Father," by Chris Tomlin came out and God used it and the words from a good friend, who happened to be a pastor, to absolutely 100% nail down the certainty of God's goodness all the time.

If you don't know the song, you should most definitely listen to it. The gist: God is a good, good Father, and it's Who He is. It's not just a characteristic of God; He is goodness.

My friend Chris talked about wrestling with the goodness of God in light of some very challenging circumstances, and essentially he had to decide if he believed if God indeed was good, because He couldn't be both good and bad at the same time.

He needed to decide once and for all if He was or wasn't. If He wasn't good, there was no point in following Him. If He was good, then he should settle it once and for all and stop asking that question.

And, I think in God's grace, He allowed me to take what I know to be true from scripture: that God keeps running after humanity to have relationship even though we continuously deny Him,

ignore Him,

and disobey Him.

And He didn't stop there. He knew we could never be good enough to have a restored relationship with Him.

So, He became the good man and lived the perfect life we couldn't live, and died the death we deserved so He could swap places with us, or transfer His account of righteousness to us and take our record of imperfection and lack of righteousness.

Good. Very good.

God's definition and God's plan.

No way would any human concoct THIS rescue plan.

Then it dawned on me: we can't define good because we don't know what good is. Our limited, finite human brains cannot begin to comprehend what, in fact, is good.

Our definition of good is skewed and bent toward what we think is good. There is no set definition of goodness by human standards. Just ask a Tarheel or Wolfpack fan and you'll get two VERY DIFFERENT definitions of good. But seriously, our emotions, amount of sleep, if we're hungry, sick, distracted, hurt … all of these factors, plus a million more, impact how humans define if something is "good." Humans aren't qualified to consistently know "good" when they see it. However, God knows what is good. And He's the only One who does know good and can measure and dispense it appropriately.

So, instead of me defining what a "good birthday" would be, I just asked Jesus to do what He knew I needed to feel seen and celebrated. And He ended up blessing me with an incredible birthday month that included multiple trips, texts, dinners and well wishes from multiple friends. I couldn't have defined what He gave me, and I'm glad I didn't settle for my lame definition of "good."

I decided that rather than asking if something is good, I should be asking, "How has Jesus been faithful this week?"

And, that one seems to be a question I can answer.

CHAPTER 73

Back to Square One, Not Quite

"Consider it pure joy whenever you face trials of various kinds, for you know the testing of your faith produces perseverance. Let perseverance finish its work so you may be complete and mature, not lacking anything."

—James 1:2-4 (NIV)

I have this tendency to think that when things don't go the way I want them to, or if I fail in some capacity, that it inherently means I'm back at "ground zero or square one" and have to start all over again. Or as the old rules in Monopoly go, it means "Do Not Pass Go, Do Not Collect $200."

A friend recently shared a similar sentiment with me about her circumstances and it dawned on me that we never really go back to "ground zero." Because Jesus orchestrates every single moment of every single day, even our failings and missteps and mistakes get factored into our stories.

What we perceive as setbacks, detours, and all-out failures, He sees as just a part of His bigger plan to make us look more like Him. He puts us in places and circumstances where we can hang in there, point people to Him, and ultimately be made complete through the gradual process of growing to look more like Jesus as we persevere in trials.

I mean, look at Abraham's life, the father of Israel. Before he was the father of Israel, he let Sarah be taken into not one, but TWO harems. David committed adultery, deception, and murder. Before he became an apostle, Paul was a Christian murderer. And these are the major failures of their lives recorded for the entire living world to read. And Jesus redeemed them. And He redeems our mistakes and uses the hardship He allows in our lives to mold us into His character.

A friend just actually sent me this text, and I thought it may encourage y'all too.

"Just thinking about you and praying for all the things going on at the moment. He is working in you such incredible things …

all for His grand purpose and design! I was reading in James ... that we suffer trials of all kinds; He uses them to make us mature, complete, not lacking anything. Such abundance in store for you, my dear."

Hangeth in there, friends. Jesus knows about this current "setback" you're experiencing, and He's going to use it to mature you and help make you complete. What a thought, to be complete! I'm certainly not there.

CHAPTER 74

Up Close & Personal With Jesus

"In this you rejoice, though now for a little while, if necessary, you have been grieved by various trials, so that the tested genuineness of your faith–more precious than gold that perishes though it is tested by fire–may be found to result in praise and glory and honor at the revelation of Jesus Christ."

—*1 Peter 1: 6-7 (ESV)*

I've been contemplating whether I should attempt to publish this collection of nuggets God has given me to share. On one hand, I'm very much like, *"Who am I to publish my story, and will anyone want to read it?"* Yet on the other hand, I've shared it with a few friends, and they, unanimously, have all said, *"Do it!"* Also, there's that still, quiet LV there too, continuing to impress on me to move forward with this, and who knows, maybe, just maybe, God will use it to plant some seeds for some new eternal siblings and encourage some others to keep going.

Now, I don't dare say, *"Oh, I've arrived at walking close with Jesus. I am the end-all-be-all of walking closely with Jesus,"* NOT by a long shot. But, I can say beyond all doubt that I am not the same woman who started writing this book ten years ago. I am a completely different and changed woman, who walks closely with Jesus. And, it would NOT be possible except for all the very hard and painful experiences He has walked me through.

Without the heartache, disappointment, failure, betrayal, loneliness, confusion, depression, anger, hurt, and loss ... I wouldn't know Jesus to be the antithesis of all of those things. I am only here today and thriving because of my beloved Jesus, and I can only say the reason why anyone would find me enjoyable to be around is because of the work He has done in my heart and life.

I can unequivocally say God is good all the time, and He is the ONLY ONE who can fill that hole in your heart and mine. If I could sit down and have coffee with you and share more of my story, I would. There's nothing I enjoy more than sharing how my Jesus cares for me and how ***He's inviting you***, reader, to experience abundant life and healing right now.

He knows everything about you and still loves you, even likes you, and wants to be in a relationship with YOU! He loved you so much that He was willing to give up His life for yours. He wants you in His family, and unlike the dysfunctional one you may have grown up with, He is the perfect Brother and Father and Husband who will NEVER leave or forsake you.

And walking closely with Him is worth whatever it takes.

CHAPTER 75

Giving Credit Where Credit Is Due

"Therefore, since we are surrounded by such a great cloud of witnesses, let us throw off everything that hinders and the sin that so easily entangles. And let us run with perseverance the race marked out for us, fixing our eyes on Jesus, the pioneer and perfecter of our faith."

—*Hebrews 12:1-2 (NIV)*

This book, and all the things captured in it, are because of Jesus. And along the way, He sent several sweet souls to encourage me, cheer me on, hug me, pray with me, cry with me, laugh with me, and project with me, among other ways. I also wouldn't be here if He hadn't sent you.

You may have texted, called, set up a coffee date, listened to me complain, shared your family and meals with me, celebrated victories with me. You know who you are, and I'm grateful for you.

I'd love to take a moment to thank every single person who made this book possible, but it would make it too long. However, I do want to thank those of you who have been faithful and who have stood beside me through the good, bad, and the ugly.

If you're looking for other great books to spur you on in your faith walk I have a very long list. However, some of the greats for me have been:

- Hinds Feet On High Places, Hannah Hurnard
- Every Bitter Thing Is Sweet, Sara Hagerty
- Unseen, Sara Hagerty
- Adore, Sara Hagerty
- The Praying Life, Paul Miller
- The Reason for Suffering, Tim Keller
- Walking with God Through Pain and Suffering, Tim Keller
- 1,000 Gifts, Ann Voskamp
- Lies Women Believe, And the Truth that Sets Them Free, Nancy Leigh DeMoss
- Heroes of the Faith, George Mueller: The Guardian of Bristol's Orphans, Geoff Benge
- Look And Live, Matt Papa
- The Path of Loneliness, Elizabeth Elliot
- Suffering is Never for Nothing, Elizabeth Elliot
- Shattered Dreams, Larry Crabb
- The Insanity of God, Nik Ripkin
- The Emotionally Destructive Marriage, Leslie Vernick

Epilogue

After getting some input from a wise and more mature woman in the faith, I decided it would be good to point out a few things about my journey which I allude to, but don't necessarily dive into.

If you have the impression that I figured this out all on my own, that could not be further from the truth.

I had an army of support over the last twenty years, and I still do. And countless efforts were made to try and bring redemption to our marriage. From pastors to friends, to couples' counselors, to retreats and specialty conferences ... Many efforts and experts attempted to help.

My position was and still is, that God intends marriage to be permanent. Before I made the painful decision to separate, I didn't fully understand the provisions God had made in His Word to enable wives to separate. On some level, I think I believed the most holy thing I could do would be to stay no matter what. Yet, as I prayed and considered if I should separate, which became unavoidable, my pastor gave me some of the most valuable wisdom from the Word, which helped me see God did not view separation as sin. And it could be a tool to bring safety, boundaries, and clarity if circumstances warrant it.

First, he pointed out the Bible doesn't contain instructions on how to sin. However, it clearly contains instructions on how to separate properly in instances that require it (1 Cor 7 ESV). Instructions on how to separate rightly helped underscore God doesn't view it as sin.

Second, he compassionately showed me God created marriage to be a metaphor to point to Christ and the church. His metaphor doesn't supersede the safety of and care for His children.

Third, he reminded me I would give an account to the King of the universe about how I lived my life. With that knowledge, he encouraged me to be convinced in my mind what my answer would be.

Knowing the reality that I will encounter many people with many perspectives on divorce, he encouraged me to have that answer settled just like Paul encouraged the Roman believers to be convinced in their own minds about eating meat that had been sacrificed to idols.

"One person esteems one day as better than another, while another esteems all days alike. Each one should be fully convinced in his own mind."

Without that answer being nailed down, he warned that I'd be vulnerable to falling into an emotional spiral should I hear a future sermon on the topic or be judged by a fellow believer. In everything he shared with me, he never once said, "You have to do this. Or you should do that." He very wisely opened the Word in front of me and entrusted God to lead me, and it steadied me as I moved forward.

If you find yourself in a similar situation, or another hard situation, I cannot emphasize how important being connected to a Bible-believing and compassionate community in the local church will be for you. Apart from the many godly men and women who attempted to help, I am certain despair would have engulfed me.

You might be tempted to go it alone and keep whatever broken thing hidden. I urge you to find at least one mature and wise believer to share your struggle with and help you walk the journey in front of you. And I know many who, because they brought their brokenness into the light, found healing, redemption, and restoration. That could be you.

Lastly, the last book on my reading list served as a solid resource to help me make sense of what I experienced. If you think you may be in an emotionally-abusive relationship, I strongly encourage you to read it.

**May Jesus draw you to Him,
as He has drawn me.**

Melissa Curtin

About the Author

Melissa Curtin never imagined herself as a writer, but thanks to a keen professor who insisted on active verbs and banished passive voice, she found her knack for putting words together. Mixing a bit of humor and tangible real-world examples, Melissa gives readers a glimpse into her story and shares hope for even the hardest circumstances. At the end of the day, her ultimate desire - encourage people and point them to Jesus through her writing.

Beyond words, Melissa loves to create things, whether it's crafting furniture for her home or crafting sentences for her book. Outdoorsy and sporty, she finds solace in nature and enjoys DIY projects...except for painting trim. Her favorite moments are spent with family and friends, sharing laughter and making memories.

Melissa's dream, if Jesus allows it, would be to write and speak. Having experienced restoration herself, she longs to help free more captives from believing their past pains and failures can only lead to dashed dreams and brokenness. Despite the warfare she's encountered on this journey, she believes in the importance of her mission, guided by far more reasons than she can begin to comprehend.